Carnations

Carnations

Perpetual-flowering Carnations,
Borders and Pinks

Steven Bailey

BLANDFORD

Blandford

an imprint of
Cassell
Artillery House, Artillery Row
London SW1P 1RT

First published 1982
First paperback edition, revised, 1990

**British Library Cataloguing in Publication
Data**
Bailey, Steven
  Carnations: perpetual-flowering carnations,
  borders and pinks. – Rev. ed.
  1. Gardens. Perpetual-flowering carnations.
  Cultivation
  I. Title
  635.9′33152

  ISBN 0-7137-2160-X

Distributed in the United States by
Sterling Publishing Co., Inc.,
387 Park Avenue South, New York, NY 10016-
8810

Distributed in Australia by
Capricorn Link (Australia) Pty Ltd
PO Box 665, Lane Cove, NSW 2066

Printed in Great Britain by
The Bath Press, Avon

Contents

Foreword to the 1982 edition

Mr Steven Bailey's very successful book on carnations has been revised to bring us up-to-date in these fast moving times, and I am honoured to be invited again to write a Foreword to it. Having known Mr Bailey for more than thirty years, and having admired his work and experience, I can be sure that this new book will be a great addition to the literature already available, and another step forward in British horticulture.

The perpetual-flowering carnation, being a plant which flowers the whole year round, is becoming more and more popular among amateur gardeners in their smaller greenhouses and this popularity will, I am sure, increase in the years ahead. The author's vast practical experience and knowledge are brought together in one book for the guidance and help of other carnation enthusiasts and growers everywhere. The book deals with all aspects of carnation growing and includes a guide to cultivars and a calendar to help us the year through. Sections on border carnations and pinks have been added.

Mr Bailey is a leading exhibitor at many of the prominent flower shows in various parts of the country and many thousands of people have been permitted to see the superb quality of his blooms, and have admired the tasteful way in which they have been staged. We at Shrewsbury value the contribution he makes to the Shrewsbury Musical and Floral Fête each year.

Having gained knowledge from the book myself, I am confident that it will find a place on the book shelves of many gardeners, professionals and amateur growers alike, and it has my best wishes for the success it so well deserves.

Percy Thrower

Preface

Prompted by the many conflicting views on the skill, knowledge
and experience, as well as the 'special' soils and greenhouses required for successful growing of perpetual-flowering carnations,
I have endeavoured in this book to explain in simple language
the culture of perpetual-flowering carnations, as well as hardy
border carnations and hardy garden pinks. Because perpetual-
flowering carnations are all-year-round plants and are mainly
grown in glasshouses, their culture is given greater prominence
in Part I of this book. Border carnations and pinks require far
less attention, only flower during the summer months, and are
much easier subjects to deal with. Their cultivation is described
in Part II. The origins and development of perpetual-flowering
carnations, borders and pinks are outlined at the beginning of
each relevant section. Part III gives descriptions of the cultivars
illustrated in the colour section.

My idea is to instil confidence and give encouragement to
those who have always wanted to try to grow a few plants for
simple enjoyment and pastime after admiring the wonderful
exhibits at various horticultural shows. I do not say that it is as
simple as all that to grow specimen blooms suitable for the show
bench, nor could I explain in a few simple words the method of
cultivation and the experience necessary to attain a perfection
which has taken me almost a lifetime to acquire.

Nevertheless, to grow a few plants, anything from a dozen to
fifty or even a hundred, and derive an unlimited amount of
pleasure from doing so, is within the reach of everyone, and with
this in mind I have written this book.

Steven Bailey

Acknowledgements

The publishers gratefully acknowledge the following for providing illustrations for this book: Robin Fletcher (pp. 13, 34, 42, 53, 87, 113 left and right, 117 and 162); F. Pratten and Co. Ltd (p. 21); Edenlite Greenhouses Ltd (p. 26); Humex Ltd (pp. 49 and 83); Glasshouse Crops Research Institute (p. 109); Plant Protection Ltd (pp. 121 and 135); George E. Hyde (p. 128); Imperial Chemical Industries Ltd (p. 131). The colour photographs on pp. 93–108 are by Steven Bailey and Robin Fletcher.

Part I
Perpetual-Flowering Carnations

Introduction

However beautiful the border carnation, the pink or any other member of the dianthus family may be, none holds that charm and exhilarating beauty which the perpetual-flowering carnation possesses. Certainly there is great beauty in the border carnation, the tiny dianthus alpine or even the common Sweet William (*Dianthus barbatus*). In their correct setting they enhance any garden or rockery. What cheer a perpetual-flowering carnation can bring, however, during the sombre and dreary winter days when one enters a greenhouse, however small, filled with these plants in full flower—especially when they are the newer cultivars with their splendid habit, long erect stems, and with such a wide range of colour in their so well-formed blooms.

Since the introduction of the cultivar 'William Sim', which came over from the United States around the year 1947, the standard of carnations has changed a good deal. This cultivar and its 'sports' can be found the world over in commercial establishments as well as among amateur growers. I have never known any cultivar to have made such an impact on the cultivation of any flower in the many years I have been associated with the growing of carnations, and the sports which have resulted from 'William Sim' are too numerous to mention.

It is claimed that the present-day perpetual-flowering carnation originated from a bush perpetual-flowering strain found among *Dianthus caryophyllus*. Almost everyone knows that the carnation is frequently referred to as the 'Divine' flower, but this is equally true of the sweet william or any of the many species of the genus *Dianthus*.

The carnation is a very ancient flower which was known for centuries before the Christian era. It was a native in the temperate regions of Europe and Asia and to a lesser extent North Africa. It was common in France and Italy. Botanically, all carnations are referred to as *Dianthus caryophyllus*, although *caryophyllus* is but one of several hundred species of the genus *Dianthus*, and there are a great many races and classes of carnations. A detailed study of this subject is very complicated

11

and more than a little confusing. I will therefore not bore the reader with all the data which I have read and found in the earliest reports on our subject but will report briefly what generally are the accepted facts.

The perpetual-flowering carnation owes its origin to at least two *Dianthus* species, namely *D. caryophyllus* and *D. sinensis*. The history of this type is reputed to have begun in the city of Lyons in France about 1830. Centuries of hybridisation and interbreeding produced new species and fixed types. During the early part of the nineteenth century, the Remontant Carnation was produced in France. This type was winter-flowering and produced blooms of greater substance. It is claimed that a well-known French gardener, Monsieur Dalmais, was mainly responsible for its creation. Stocks of these carnations were eventually produced and were imported into the United States during 1852, and the first American cultivar was introduced in 1858. A well-known American cultivar was raised from these French originals and was named 'Daybreak'. In 1895 Mr Peter Fisher, then one of the leading American pioneers, raised the famous cultivar 'Mrs T. W. Lawson' by crossing 'Daybreak' with a Continental cultivar named 'Van Leeuwen'. 'Mrs T.W. Lawson' was truly perpetual, and its strong habit of growth compensated for a lack of form in its large cerise and serrated flowers.

In the meantime stock from France had been sent to England as well as some of the latest seedlings of the American cultivars, and some of our leading growers very soon produced some remarkable seedlings such as 'Winter Cheer', a bright scarlet, 'Miss Joliffe', pale rose, and others. The American seedling 'Mrs T. W. Lawson' also came to England; and a well-known raiser of that time, Mr Alfred Smith, crossed 'Lawson' with 'Winter Cheer' and produced the famous cultivar 'Britannia', a scarlet.

It can justly be claimed that 'Britannia' was the forerunner of many famous British cultivars. Equally famous American cultivars would be 'Enchantress', 'Spectrum', 'Topsy' and several others which contributed in many respects to the advance in breeding in subsequent years.

Amongst the British raisers, the greatest must surely be the late Carl Englemann, a German immigrant to this country who finally established the world-wide known establishment at

12

A commercial crop of perpetual-flowering carnations.

Saffron Walden in Essex; the late Montague Allwood, affection-
ately known by his many friends as 'Monty', who together with
his two brothers, George and Edward, started and controlled his
famous nurseries in Wivelsfield, Sussex, until his death in 1959;
and to a lesser extent, the firm of Stuart Low & Co. of Enfield,
Middlesex.

Carl Englemann raised cultivars such as the outstanding 'Lady
Northcliffe', which although only of medium size was the
favourite of many commercial growers, due to its abundant production and good keeping qualities; 'Saffron', which was
introduced in 1916 and was the best yellow I can remember;
'Cupid' (1920), a rosy salmon of good size; 'Dorcas', the crimson
which was awarded the George Monro Cup in London in 1927.

Some of the best I remember from Monty Allwood are
'Wivelsfield White' (1915), 'Robert Allwood', a large, bright
scarlet, 'Mary Allwood' (1913), 'Wivelsfield Crimson'; these are
only a few of the older cultivars. There were, however, dozens of
new cultivars arriving each year, for the chances of improvement
were great in comparison with the opportunity we have today of

creating something worthwhile with the standard we have now reached.

'Baroness de Brienen' must certainly be mentioned as one of the earliest and best known of the achievements of Stuart Low & Co. It was a beautiful and very large shell pink which unfortunately was best in the summer. This cultivar came out in 1912. 'Eileen Low' was another from their Enfield nursery. I think the most famous must be the clear large white, 'White Pearl', which was the favourite of George V and which His Majesty frequently wore as a buttonhole.

My personal interest and efforts in hybridising commenced at a somewhat later date, encouraged by the well-known chrysanthemum breeder and grower of the period 1920–26, Keith Luxford of Sawbridgeworth, Hertsfordshire, in whose employment I was at that time, in charge of the carnation houses on that nursery. It was some years, however, before I attained any measure of success; in actual fact it was not until after the war in 1947 that I had some seedlings which showed promise. The first, 'Bailey's Masterpiece', was introduced from our Sway nurseries in 1948, followed by 'Bailey's Apricot' and 'Bailey's Pride' in 1949, all of which continue to be grown and are still being awarded prizes in show bloom classes.

Since these early days I have indeed been fortunate in adding further new cultivars such as 'Bailey's Superb', 'Bailey's Supreme' (1951) and, more recently, that well-known and almost perfect carnation 'Bailey's Splendour' (pale pink), and its attractive sport, 'Rose Splendour', an almost fluorescent cerise. Quite recent introductions are 'Icecap', a pure white, especially good for winter production, 'Bailey's Amarillo', a pastel cream shade with delightful clove scent and, one of the many sports we have introduced, 'Fragrant Rose', the only sport to date of that well-known cultivar 'Fragrant Ann', which gained us the Daily Mail Gold Trophy for the best scented carnation at the London Show the first time it was exhibited.

We would like to think that over the years we, too, have contributed something to the development of the carnation and the advance of cultivars and cultivation in general, but it will be up to future generations to evaluate our work.

Another famous cultivar was 'Laddie' and its sport 'Red

Laddie', raised in America and imported and introduced by Carl Englemann.

During the period 1915–20 the carnation was often referred to as the 'American tree carnation'. No doubt this was due to the fact that at that time the new perpetual hybrids coming over from the States possessed a taller habit and, being truly perpetual, were often grown for three or four years as a commercial crop, during which time they attained 1.5-1.8 m in height.

It is often our experience, when attending to our specialised groups of carnation blooms at shows all over the country, to hear remarks passed by one or another admirer: 'I wish we could grow a few of these, but then, we have no special heating in our greenhouse', or 'I have had a go but it was no use'. When tempted to enter such conversation it has often been most difficult to explain that it is only a moderate and certainly not a high temperature that is needed, nor a specially-constructed greenhouse, but any ordinary small, or even home-made little place in which the finest plants could be grown.

I tell my listener that a temperature of say 4–7°C (40–45°F) is all that is needed, and if in summer adequate ventilation to the top as well as the side of the greenhouse can be given there should be no reason why he should not be able to grow quite good plants with the most pleasing results.

We have proved for ourselves that the old idea of high and lofty houses are not the only suitable carnation houses, and I know of at least one very experienced commercial grower who would tell you that he grows most remarkable crops in really small and low houses such as are normally used for cucumbers on commercial nurseries.

I hasten to add that, in my opinion, the greatest advantage is an abundance of light. This is one of the main ingredients for success with carnations. It is also one of the major reasons why over more recent years the development of the glasshouse industry has been concentrated along the south coast of England between Brighton in the east and the county of Dorset in the west. More and more glass is being erected in this area, which is now also spreading to the Isle of Wight. It was this light factor which decided me to come to Sway, halfway between Bourne-

15

mouth and Southampton, as far back as 1937, in order to provide the ideal environment for growing carnations to perfection.

The aim should be to learn and understand the requirements of the carnation plant, and the better acquainted you become with these facts the more enthusiastic you will be. In the following chapters the most important points of general cultivation and care of the plant are covered. I have made my explanations as simple as possible as this book is intended to be a useful reference for the real beginners as well as the more experienced. So let us start with the culture of perpetual-flowering carnations and trust that what follows will help both beginners and more competent growers, in the hope that all will gain further knowledge which will help them to even greater enjoyment and success.

The Greenhouse

As already mentioned, the most simply constructed greenhouse is suitable, provided it is fitted with adequate ventilation (in the top as well as both sides of the house if it is of the span type, and at one side of a lean-to).

Construction

As carnations require all the light possible, especially during the winter when days are short and often dull, the structure of the house should not be too clumsy if built of timber, and the rafters should be spaced at least sufficiently far apart to take a pane of glass 46 cm wide.

Wherever possible my preference would always be for sheets or panes of glass 60 × 60 cm. The rafters would be spaced approximately 60 cm apart and there would be a lesser number of overlaps, all of which tends to make the house lighter.

It is common belief that the greater the overlap given by over-lapping one pane of glass over the lower one, the less chance there will be for drip. This, however, is a mistaken idea. I would never allow more than 6 mm. Not only is this adequate but it also avoids dust and algae collecting between the two sheets of glass, which besides looking unsightly is detrimental to hygiene. Fungi collect at such places, and furthermore it causes unnecessary shade which is not beneficial to the plants, especially carnations which enjoy all possible light, particularly during the winter.

The best span roof would have a pitch of approximately 33°. A 152 × 38 mm ridgeboard with a glazing groove along each side is standard pattern. Rafters such as are used by commercial growers are 76 × 38 mm with a 6-mm glazing groove or rabbet each side. The end rafters are usually of heavier timber but 76 × 76 mm would be sufficient.

I would insist on fixing a standard capping horizontally on the ridge which would protect the ridgeboard and at the same time cover the hinged edge of the roof ventilators. The capping should not be too wide and 102 × 25 mm thick would be all that is needed.

Wall plate or cill	End of corner mullion	End rafters
1	2	3
76 × 127 mm	76 × 102 mm	76 × 76 mm
Top or eve plate and dripboard	Ridgeboard	Rafters
5 / 4	6	7
25 × 64 mm / 76 × 102 mm	38 × 152 mm	38 × 76 mm
Intermediate mullion	Transom or side vent hanging rail	Vent seats
8	9	10
76 × 102 mm	76 × 76 mm	38 × 64 mm
Capping	Door frame	Half glass door
11	A	B
25 × 102 mm		
2-pane roof ventilator	3-pane roof ventilator	Over door vent
C	D	E
When using glass 610 × 610 mm	When using glass 457 × 508 mm	2 – 305 × 610 mm

Fig. 1 *Prepared and moulded timbers required for the construction of a greenhouse.*

18

Fig. 2 An ideal carnation house. The erection specification for timbers as detailed in Fig. 1.

Roof ventilators are obtainable in standard size. If the glass size which is intended for use is 457 × 508 mm, the standard ventilator will be so made that it will take three such panes giving an opening of approximately 1.5 m × 508 mm. If, however, a 610 × 610 mm pane is decided on, a roof ventilator taking only two panes should be used.

Even the smallest greenhouse should have at least one ventilator on each side of the ridge. For the longer house, I suggest roof ventilators placed alternately along each side. This in actual fact would mean that between each three-pane ventilator there are three fixed panes of glass, or in the case of the larger pane and using a two-pane ventilator only, two fixed panes between each ventilator spaced along the roof.

So often the ventilation provided for the smaller amateur greenhouses is far from adequate. Frequently one sees a greenhouse measuring 2 × 2.5 m supplied with only one ventilator at one side of the ridge only, and this not of adequate size.

Apart from the fact that this will not provide adequate ventilation, you could not always open this ventilator if the wind happened to be towards that side of the roof. Bearing in mind that if only a little ventilation is required the leeside only should be opened, if this one ventilator happens to be on the wind-side you should not open this side on a cold windy day. Therefore, the obvious answer is that the greenhouse should have at least one ventilator each side of the ridge.

Our calculations in connection with 'adequate' ventilation for any greenhouse suggest that ventilator openings totalled together should equal $\frac{1}{6}$ of the ground area covered by the greenhouse. Take, for example, a greenhouse measuring 3.6 m long and 2.4 m wide; the area would be 3.6 × 2.4 = 8.64 m². The total ventilator openings of this greenhouse should be 8.64 ÷ 6 = 1.44 m². If each ventilator covers an opening of, say, 0.6 × 0.6 m = 0.36 m², one would need at least four such ventilators in order to provide adequate ventilation, two of which could be positioned each side of the ridge, one just to right of centre, the other on the opposite side just left of centre. The other two should be positioned in the glass side wall, one to each side.

As ventilation plays an important part at all times of the year, and especially during warm summer weather in order to reduce temperature, it would be well worth while, if you are erecting your own greenhouse, to allow for two ventilators in addition to those already mentioned, one over the door in one gable end, and the other at the opposite gable end.

Remember that warm air rises so, therefore, in order that warm air may be allowed to escape freely so as to allow cool air from outside to enter and thus create air buoyancy and movement, the gable end ventilators would be best placed as high up in the gables as is possible (*see* Figs. 1 and 2).

The design and orientation of the greenhouse are of paramount importance, because within this aspect are covered the all-important points of light transmission and ventilation. Light transmission and availability is by far the most important point, because quantity and quality of blooms is determined by this, especially during the late autumn and winter period. It is also for this sole reason that I would prefer the largest possible pane of glass for glazing the greenhouse. I would never use glass of less than 610 × 610 mm and even occasionally use panes measuring 610 × 1220 mm. The thickness of such glass will naturally be greater than for smaller panes.

With regard to orientation, it was always considered to be correct to site a span-roof greenhouse running north to south. In recent years it has been shown that there are numerous advantages in siting the structure from east to west. It has been shown authoritatively that a greenhouse running from east to west will, during the winter time, transmit 40 per cent more light than a

The Provident greenhouse, with a wooden frame. Note the provision of adequate ventilation with ventilators on both sides of the ridge, as well as the sides.

similar house sited from north to south. This alone is sufficient to recommend this new approach, but there is another equally important point in its favour: with one side of the roof facing south, only that one side of the roof requires shading during summer when shading may be called for, thus reducing the amount of work as well as reducing the amount of shading material required.

If shading material of a semi-permanent nature is used (and there are a number of proprietary brands available) so as to alleviate the necessity of renewing the shading after each shower of rain, it will obviously become rather dark in the greenhouse during a dull spell of weather. Here is another advantage of shading only one side of the roof, since it will be less dark than if both sides had to be shaded.

The least expensive and in my opinion the most effective material for shading is whiting mixed with raw linseed oil, which, after water has been added, forms an ideal emulsion which can be sprayed on to the outside of the glass with most spraying syringes. Beware, however, that you use only whiting such as is used for making putty. Never use lime, especially on wooden structures. This would harm the paintwork, and if allowed to penetrate into the wood would make future repainting very nearly useless.

Be certain, too, that you mix the whiting first with the linseed oil (old engine oil, too, has been used with success); only after thorough mixing can water be added to bring it to the required thick milky solution. This type of shading becomes transparent when wet and therefore allows more light to enter on a rainy day.

It must be remembered that dirty glass hampers and reduces light transmission. Average dirty greenhouse glass reduces light availability often by as much as 10 or 15 per cent, and in the winter when light is already so much less than ideal for carnations, it is important that it is not reduced still further because of dirty glass.

Routine washing down of the exterior surface of all glass is, therefore, fully justified and should be attended to during autumn and the winter period in particular. (There is of course no finer glass cleanser than a good downfall of snow—its sliding action down the slope of the glass will remove all dirt.)

22

Adequate ventilation has already been dealt with, but in addition an electric fan will be a worthwhile investment. In the larger greenhouses, one or two fans extracting air from the house can often be a means of improving what otherwise could well be inadequate ventilation. The fans, too, will help so much in air movement, and thereby reduce the risk of fungal diseases considerably.

The commercial grower will be looking for the possibility of from 50 to 60 air changes per hour, in order to provide the best possible conditions within the greenhouse on a hot summer day. As far as is possible and practical, the amateur grower would be well advised to approach this as closely as is within his power and means. A fan or fans should be adequate to provide an air change of $7-10$ m^3 per minute per m^2 of floor area.

The sides of the greenhouse, depending on its size, must be at least half glass and the remainder of solid construction. The lower part could be made of timber, asbestos or brick. To give adequate headroom along the eaves you should aim for 610 mm of solid construction, of which the best is brick on a 76 × 228 mm foundation, and 102 mm of glass.

The brick sides having been erected, a timber wall plate 127 × 76 mm of the conventional pattern is placed on a bed of mortar.

Besides this are needed corner mullions and intermediate mullions, in between which the side ventilators are placed. Side ventilators are by no means a superfluous item. Even when purchasing a ready-made greenhouse, always insist that besides roof ventilators there are also side ventilators to every 3 m of greenhouse length on both sides. Do not accept the manufacturer's or salesman's assurance that side ventilators are not really necessary. During winter they would of course not be used but they are absolutely essential in summer. Do not be tempted to make do by leaving the greenhouse door open as an alternative to side ventilators. An open door causes a draught directly over the soil and should be avoided.

Also required is an eave plate, the horizontal timber in between the wall plate and which the rafter and mullions are nailed. The underside of the eave plate should have a glazing groove for glazing the sides. Finally, the drip bar must not be omitted.

For all construction work always use galvanised nails and brass

23

screws. True, it will add slightly to the cost, but never be tempted to economise by using ordinary wire nails or steel screws. Invariably, such nails or screws will, after a time, start to rust, and consequently rot will start in the timber around them. It has been my experience that galvanised or 'sheradised' nails, brass or 'sheradised' screws do prolong the life of the greenhouse and are well worthwhile.

A few extra lengths of rafter for the ends will be needed, and either one or two half-glazed greenhouse doors with doorframes, depending on whether a door at one end or both ends is required.

Before starting building work it is advisable to treat all timber with green Cuprinol (SQD); and a double application is worth every effort and expense. For glazing use a good linseed oil putty and 19-mm brass brads.

Metal-framed Greenhouses

Much can be said for the modern metal-framed greenhouses, either in steel or aluminium, as the framework is so light all possible light is admitted. In purchasing this type one should make sure that it is provided with sufficient ventilation. I have seen many of these metal-framed houses at horticultural shows and elsewhere, and there are some in which the ventilation has been somewhat overlooked. These are, in my opinion, not suitable for perpetual-flowering carnation growing. Although it is argued that metal houses are much colder than wooden structures, I do not think that the difference is so great as to be detrimental. If one considers the great surface of glass on a greenhouse compared with the actual surface of metal or wood where heat loss can occur, it will readily be seen that the heat loss through the glass is very great and that the little difference in metal or wood surface will be of small consequence. Personally I would not have any objection to a metal house for that reason alone. An aluminium glasshouse would be my particular choice.

Another point worth mentioning regarding metal houses, and which should be carefully noted when inspecting such a house with the intention of making a purchase, is that with some structures of this type there are large apertures between the overlaps of the glass. It is very important to avoid these for two reasons: one is that there is a considerable loss of heat in cold weather as well as draughts; secondly, if trouble with pests occurs, as it often does, these houses do not lend themselves to the use of the present-day smoke generators or fumigants, as the loss of the fumes would be so great as to make it impossible to build up the required concentration.

Heating

A regular temperature maintained in the greenhouse is definitely a requirement which must not be overlooked. There are many forms of heating apparatus now on the market for the amateur greenhouse. Paraffin heaters are quite suitable, provided that they do not emit fumes or smoke.

For a greenhouse say 15 × 5 m or more, a small boiler such as the Robin Hood, the Ideal, and many other makes, is the most usual, but regular attention must be paid to the cleaning of the fire—seven days each week as well as filling every night, which sometimes is not so convenient.

For an amateur's greenhouse, from the smallest to the largest, an electric heater, thermostatically controlled, would be ideal. After setting the thermostat at the required temperature nothing further need be done. When the temperature in the house rises above the predetermined degree the thermostat cuts off and no fuel or current is used, but as soon as the temperature drops below it the heat is switched on, and a regular temperature is maintained. There is, however, one danger which in some districts can be troublesome, and that is the cutting of the current at the main due to power failure or a service breakdown. Fortunately, repairs are quickly effected and in most areas this problem is not a serious one.

A more recent revelation in greenhouse heating is hot air heating. Such a system is to be recommended in particular for carnations. The air from the greenhouse is drawn in by means of a fan and passed over an electric grid which heats the air, from where it is conducted through perforated polythene tubing. This tubing can be hung overhead or along the walls wherever it is required. Here again the temperature is completely thermostatically controlled. The fan, however, can be manually controlled if desired and can be used for air circulation alone. This is a great advantage during the summer, and helps a good deal to

The Eden greenhouse is ideal for carnations, as it has a maximum amount of light penetration and ample ventilation. Erection on a plinth of block or brickwork 30–45 cm high to give extra light would be better still.

avoid stagnation and thereby fungal infection such as mildew, *Botrytis*, and so on.

With solid fuel boilers, of course, the boiler has to be stoked and attended to during the entire 24 hours, and fuel consumption is continuous. Many commercial growers have changed over to oil-fired boilers. These are more or less automatic and the control is by thermostat; only occasional attention is required provided, of course, that there is an adequate supply of oil fuel in the tank. A small oil-fired boiler should also be given consideration by the smaller grower.

Electric heating will maintain a far more constant temperature and does not require the attention that boilers do, whatever type they may be. It is advisable to consult a good electrical engineer on the question of electrically heating greenhouses.

If carnations are grown in a completely cold greenhouse, very few flowers, if any, will open during winter; many will damp off, although only heavy frost would kill the plants.

If, for financial or other reasons, the above suggestion for heating cannot be adopted, it would be possible to provide some temperature by means of ingenious use of an ordinary fumeless oil heater. There are greenhouse oil heaters available which will burn reasonably well for 48 hours on one filling of a good paraffin oil. Such a heater would be sufficient to keep frost out of the greenhouse and in many cases would provide a temperature of 3 or 5°C (5 or 10°F) above outside conditions.

There are varying opinions as to how much heat is required to grow carnation plants successfully, but anyone with any experience at all will readily agree that cool-grown material is of better quality and has more vigour than the warmer-grown plants. If a moderately high temperature is kept during winter, a larger quantity of bloom is obtained; if grown cool, the number of blooms per plant is reduced. Those which are cut, however, are of more substance and better colour. Besides, plants thus grown maintain their vigour and do not give that sickly appearance during spring, so often noticeable with plants grown in a forcing kind of temperature.

I would definitely say that a winter temperature over 7°C (45°F) is detrimental to the well-being of the carnation plant; although not an impossible proposition for a well-experienced grower, who can, by feeding correctly, to some extent prevent the softening of the plant. I would therefore advise the beginner to aim for a temperature of 4–7°C (40–45°F) if possible, especially during prolonged spells of dull weather, when it would be advisable to lower the temperature two degrees or so.

In the south of England it is not uncommon to overwinter plants in the greenhouse without any artificial heat at all; even if the temperature should drop to 1 or 2°C (33 or 35°F) I would not worry unduly. During a recent winter, when conditions were mild for the time of the year, we did not light any boilers, with the exceptions of the propagating house fire and those for houses where the young plants are potted into the first pots. All bloom houses were grown entirely cold, and with the approach of the following spring it was very noticeable how these plants stood up to the April sunshine without any embarrassment or signs of flagging.

Needless to say, the number of blooms we cut during that winter was below average, but it was also our experience that far fewer 'seconds' were found in the sorting prior to sending blooms to market than was usual. At the same time such plants, cool-grown, with ventilation when possible, are more resistant to insect infestation and are not so subject to disease.

The ideal winter temperature then would be about 4°C (40°F), and do not hesitate to give ventilation on all suitable occasions, always avoiding draughts.

If suitable heating is installed, remember that it is not only used for maintaining a temperature around 4–7°C (40–45°F). Especially during autumn and in particular from late September throughout October and November, a thermostatically controlled heating system might well not come into operation when the outside temperature is such that the thermometer in the greenhouse does not fall below 4 or 7°C (40 or 45°F), yet it might be advisable to provide some measure of artificial heat to maintain a dry atmosphere. Humidity during that time of the year can be very high, causing condensation on the inside of the greenhouse glass. Such conditions are harmful to carnation plants and blooms. It would be advisable to give adequate ventilation and provide some form of heating to encourage air circulation around the plants. This point is frequently overlooked, yet it is very important.

Borders, Beds and Raised Benches
As I shall be dealing with pots and potting later on I will only describe the beds or bench system now. In both cases adequate drainage is essential.

It is frequently asked what commercial growers mean by 'beds'. I will briefly explain as follows: timber boards, asbestos strips or similar material some 15–18 cm wide are set up on the general ground level of the greenhouse to provide a receptacle or trough which can be filled with compost in which the plants are planted out. Approximately 25 cm below the top of these sides, a good layer of brick rubble or clinker is placed to give the necessary drainage, leaving at least 18 cm depth below the top of the sides to take the soil mixture in which the carnations are grown.

Beds with solid bases are also very popular. All our commercial beds are of the solid base type. I prefer to make these bases of

28

concrete some 5 cm thick and shaped like a shallow 'V', i.e. slightly sloping from the sides to the centre which is some 5 or 8 cm lower than the sides. Place a 5-cm land drain, a half round tile or even a length of half round galvanised guttering upside down along the centre of the bed in the lowest part of the V through the entire length of the bed, for a drainage channel. A gentle fall, approximately 2.5 cm in every 3 m run of bed should be allowed for when laying the concrete, to give the surplus water a free outlet at the lowest end of the bed.

The line of land drain or guttering should be covered with approximately 2.5 cm of 2 cm washed shingle to ensure that the drainage is satisfactory.

The amateur, who may wish to make a similar bed, but less permanent and obviously less costly, could well accomplish a satisfactory result by using a heavy gauge polythene in place of concrete.

Where the bed is to be made, the soil will have to be shaped and rolled so that, after placing the polythene sheeting in position to form the base, the bed is V-shaped as outlined previously, and the centre of the V will slope to one end to allow the surplus water to run away freely.

After shaping the base and before placing the polythene in position, stakes are driven into the soil along both sides of the beds against which are placed the side-boards, 15–20 cm in width. These could be wooden planks or asbestos strips. The polythene is then placed in position to form the base of the bed so that the edges of the polythene come up to the top of the side-boards, forming a complete and isolated trough to hold the compost in which to grow the plants.

We shall presume that the soil in the greenhouse is a good fibrous loam, in which case this can be used to fill the beds. Otherwise a good loam with plenty of fibre has to be brought in. As quite a number of ingredients have to be mixed with the soil, we only fill the beds to within some 5 cm from the top.

To every 4 parts of loam we add 1 part of well-decayed manure. If the soil is heavy, use horse manure, while on lighter soils farmyard or even cow manure would do equally well. On all soils it would be well to incorporate also a little mortar rubble or brick rubble to ensure an open mixture, and finally a dusting of chalk lime and a good carnation base manure, according to manufacturers' directions. Charcoal is a very good substance where soil is inclined to turn sour quickly.

The beds, thus prepared and well mixed, are ready for raking. Contrary to the old belief in treading the beds to consolidate really well, I would only press the soil along the edges of the beds with the back of the rake while levelling off and preparing for planting.

Admittedly, carnations like a fairly firm soil but after the beds have had two or three waterings they will settle down by the time the plants become established. It should be possible to plant with the fingers, instead of a trowel, making a hole to receive the soil ball of the plant as it is knocked out of the pot.

The method of benches, or raised beds, is very similar, the only exception being that these beds are raised above ground level, allowing an air space below. Naturally a base, or bottom, is required, and this can be made with concrete paving slabs, tiles, or part asbestos sheets (full sheets, 2.5 × 1.2 m cut in half lengthways).

If a raised bed is made 1.2 m wide, it is easy to make a base with asbestos sheets, 13 mm thick, cut in half lengthways, giving a strip 2.5 m long and 0.6 m wide. Place a row of bricks on edge the entire length of the proposed centre of the bed, on which one edge of the asbestos will rest, while along the sides of the bed bricks are placed at intervals of one every 30 cm on the flat. This completed, we have a base slanting from the middle to each side. Strips of asbestos 20 cm wide and 2.5 m long are now placed on top of the base to form the sides and these are held in place by stakes driven into the ground. It is not essential to secure the sides to the stakes as the soil we place in the beds will stop them from falling inwards. Ends are placed in position, and the raised bed is ready for filling with soil. The same mixture can be used as already described, but of course it is not necessary to use clinker or brick rubble as a base to provide drainage, as we shall have all the drainage we require in this type of bed.

These beds are very simple to make, yet most effective and certainly lasting. When using asbestos, however, it is best to use 10 mm thick for the sides and 13 mm for bases and not the 6 mm which normally is easier to obtain.

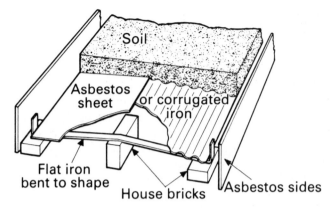

Fig. 3 Section of a raised bed.

In Fig. 3 is shown a close-up of a raised bed. Here we have used a concrete paving slab 60 × 5 cm supported by a metal bar 4 cm wide and shaped to correspond with the brick on edge in the middle and a brick placed flat at each side. To avoid the necessity of using wooden stakes to support the sides, we made the bars longer than required for the base only and bent them upwards 25 cm, thus making a support for the asbestos strips which form the sides. This is also clearly shown in Fig. 3.

The advantage of raised beds is in the easier control of moisture during the winter months. These beds also lie warmer than other beds, but the disadvantage is felt during a hot summer when they need watering a good deal more. It is with this in mind that a really good fibrous loam should be used. Soil in raised beds should also be firmer, and light treading is often necessary.

Propagation

Purchase of Plants

To begin with, the culture of perpetual-flowering carnations is the same as with any other plant, whether it be chrysanthemums, roses, or anything else. Make sure you buy the right type of stock and that it is clean and sturdy as well as free from disease.

The best growers grow 'stock plants' for the specific purpose of producing cuttings only. It has been proved beyond doubt that cuttings produced from such plants are far superior to those taken from flowering plants. Obviously when the amateur grower does his own propagation it is not possible to grow special stock plants. He should, however, select the best of the cuttings available referred to in this chapter.

Nowadays one is apt to hear a good deal also of 'cultured cuttings' which in fact means that all propagating material has been subject to laboratory tissue tests, which, in almost all cases, is beyond the scope of the small or medium-sized commercial concerns, let alone the amateur. It is certainly not necessary, and the mention of this modern technique does not need to cause any second thoughts on the part of the amateur in any way. All it implies is that the commercial carnation plant producer has, nowadays, means at his disposal whereby he can examine his stock thoroughly and, more or less, guarantee his cuttings free from any vascular disease.

From such 'cultured' stock only the very best plants are grown on to produce the ultimate multiplication stock from which cuttings and plants are supplied.

In more recent years, a good deal has been said about 'meristem cuttings' and 'heat therapy'. This technique in eliminating internal disease is even more effective and efficient than the culturing technique, and requires facilities often not possible for anyone else to supply except research and experimental laboratories. This technique, however, does ensure freedom from well-known virus diseases, such as mottle, vein mottle, ring spot and others known to affect carnations. Serious virus infection reduces production and depreciates quality of bloom,

32

sometimes to such an extent that badly infected varieties are no longer suitable for commercial purposes.

The technique is complicated, requires a high degree of skill, and a very high degree of painstaking efficiency on the part of the worker. More details of this are included in the chapter on pests and diseases.

Many are the sources of supply and equally as many are the disappointments. It may at first appear costly, but then that applies to everything we buy if quality goods are what we are looking for. Cheap shoes are easily recognised, whereas a suit of clothes of the best possible material and cut by expert cutters cannot be expected to be cheap. A cheap article could prove to be the most expensive in the long run, and this is more true than ever where purchases of cheap plants are concerned.

To commence then with the best possible plant, you should only purchase from a well-known firm, preferably from one who specialises in perpetual-flowering carnations. The owner, as well as his staff, will be experienced, and will also be most particular about selecting his stock and propagating material—so essential to maintain one's stock at the highest possible level.

Once a good stock is in your possession, you may prefer to propagate your own in the future and only make occasional purchases for the sake of acquiring some new variety you may see at one or another show, and which takes your fancy either for colour, habit, or any of the many things we like in a plant.

For the reason then of maintaining your own stock by means of propagating cuttings, it is of the utmost importance that you start with the right type of plant of a vigorous and healthy stock. It is from this simple plant that future plants will be propagated and it must be obvious that no good can be expected if the results obtained from the parent plant are not what they might have been.

A common question is: 'Is it best to buy rooted cuttings or young plants in small pots?' The answer is complicated and needs clarification. The cheapest way would naturally be to use rooted cuttings. Commercial growers always buy their new plants this way, of course, when they pot them and have the necessary facilities to house and look after them until they eventually are planted in the beds or potted on for stock. It calls,

An example of a rooted cutting.

however, for some skill, and it is only to the more experienced amateur grower that I would recommend this method of purchasing their requirements.

The best way, slightly more expensive but more certain of results, would be to purchase plants in pots, 'stopped and broken'. This term must be explained, because I recall one occasion when I submitted a quotation to a beginner and emphasised that the plants we would supply were well established and 'stopped and broken', whereupon he replied rather disgustedly that he was not prepared to accept broken plants. It means of course that all plants would have received the 'first stop' and are forming their natural 'breaks', or side shoots.

Young plants in small pots are normally available from approximately the middle of spring and come from cuttings taken during the early winter. It will be clear therefore that such plants, although delivered at a later date than rooted cuttings, are virtually the same; in actual fact they should be better, for more skilful attention has been given to them by the nurseryman who has better facilities during that tricky part of the year and thereby is able to produce a better plant than the average amateur.

Briefly, therefore, I would in most cases suggest a preference for young plants in pots, except for those who have successfully handled rooted cuttings during the period of mid-winter to early spring.

The next question is: 'Which cultivars should we order?' I find it almost impossible to give any ruling on all the colours and shades or colour combinations which are available in carnations. Tastes for colour vary so widely. To a beginner I would always suggest a 'collection', consisting of either six or twelve plants in assorted colours and cultivars which are selected by the nurseryman according to stock available.

I cannot speak on behalf of all specialists supplying carnation plants, but I would assure anyone holding the belief that 'collections' of plants and 'growers' selection' (offered at a much lower cost than list prices) must obviously be of inferior quality that they are misinformed. A good specialist who has a reputation to maintain, and is desirous of retaining the confidence which is so necessary in our industry, would not be so foolish as to offer an inferior plant to his customer even at a lower rate. Such a practice would be very short-sighted, as the horticultural plant trade depends to a very great extent on recommendations. In our own nurseries, for instance, it often happens that more plants of certain cultivars have been propagated than are required or have been ordered at a later date, and it is better to include these in collections than have them on hand until they are of no further use, even if these cultivars should be the higher priced ones.

Furthermore, orders for collections can be handled more quickly, and consequently are not charged with the same overheads as orders which have to be collected individually before despatch from the various locations on the nursery.

The amateur need never have any doubts about ordering a collection, as such. There would be such colours as white, pink, scarlet and one or two 'fancies', which to start with would be a nice assortment. At a later date it may be that one or two other cultivars would be preferred which are then ordered individually to augment the collection.

It will be realised that, at first sight of a carnation specialist's price list, the prices quoted may seem rather expensive; in fact, that is not the case, provided that good strong stock is secured. For a specialist, to maintain a first-class stock can be very expensive if he does the job correctly, and makes a real and true effort to maintain a careful selection of plants from which his cuttings are taken.

Compare prices of bedding plants, for instance a box of bedding plants for your garden; normally 18–24 small plants raised from seed, and no more time spent on them than just sowing and pricking out, mostly in unsterilised soil, may cost you 75–80p. These plants are annuals, however, and we must therefore buy a fresh supply each year; carnations, on the other hand, are different. Once a stock has been bought it is there for as long as we care to propagate from it, so long as that stock is kept healthy and clean. With an occasional purchase of a new cultivar which attracts us, to replace one which has become too old, or which we do not fancy as well, our interest in the cultivation of the perpetual-flowering carnation will grow with experience.

Finally, there are plants in 13 cm pots which can be purchased. The first impression may be that these plants are too costly, for, on average, they may cost double the price of plants in 6 or 8 cm pots. It should be remembered, however, that such plants were originally propagated at more or less the same time as those offered in the smaller pots and have had to be cared for ever since, not forgetting the actual potting-on and all it entails. Such plants are usually available from the specialists by mid-summer and throughout the late summer and autumn. Therefore the nurseryman has had the care of such plants for something like seven or eight months. Specialist care has ensured that the plants have been stopped correctly and by the time they are despatched they will be either in bud or showing their first blooms. Therefore they are certainly a very attractive proposition. A point which should also be borne in mind is that such plants will provide a supply of cuttings during the coming winter months which could be propagated and thus produce the new young plants for the following year. One such plant in a 13 cm pot, producing blooms throughout the winter from the time they are received, could, in addition, produce four or five new plants by the end of the winter. It is not difficult to see that this may well be the most economic proposition of all.

Whatever is decided upon, I cannot emphasise enough the importance of ensuring that plants purchased are from a firm which specialises in carnations as, so often, plants of inferior origin cause sufficient disappointment to cause the grower to lose interest in the culture of carnations; whereas had he started with plants from a reputable source, which possessed vigour, good health, etc, his interest would have increased.

Cuttings and Seeds

The usual way, in fact the only way, to ensure true reproduction of cultivars is by means of cuttings. We are often asked for a packet of seeds of this or that cultivar and no doubt many think this is the way in which perpetual-flowering carnation plants are produced.

These carnations can be and are originally grown from seeds; at my nursery we grow many thousands of seedlings each year. These are not for flower production but solely for the raising of new cultivars. Crossings are made each summer in an endeavour to bring out the better qualities of one cultivar and merge them with another. Before we can see the result of our predetermined crossing, we have to wait a complete year before the seedling thus obtained will show its first blooms and which, we hope, will be something new, or at least an improvement on what we already grow. It may all seem very interesting and very simple, but disappointments are many. One cannot know what results to expect from perpetual-flowering carnation seedlings; in many cases a large percentage of them may be single blooms. By this I mean a small bloom on a very long stem as a rule, with no more than four to six petals—an absolutely useless article.

It is clear then that carnations grown from seed are not necessarily reproductions of the actual parent plant. In fact, from one seedpod as many as 40–60 seeds may be obtained which, when sown, could easily result in all the plants thus produced being different in one way or another. Some may be very tall; others dwarf and bushy. It is by careful planning and working to a predetermined sort of pedigree programme that it is possible to raise some new cultivar worthy of registration.

To maintain a stock of a certain cultivar with its own particular habit, character of plant, and colour of bloom, we must propagate from cuttings. Only by this method can we reproduce a cultivar possessing the identical characteristics, substance, colour and vigour, although by careless selection of cuttings vigour especially can easily be lost.

In conclusion, therefore, I would suggest that carnations are grown from seed only after you have established a healthy stock of well known and proved cultivars and their culture is well understood and appreciated. Only then would I say that sowing seed could provide an added attraction and interest. From the foregoing and more particularly now, since the standard of present-day cultivars is very high, it will give a good deal of disappointment, but it could well be possible to be fortunate enough to find perhaps one which has outstanding merits. After all, I can think of one cultivar of recent years, namely, 'Fragrant Ann,' which was a seedling raised by an amateur in Derbyshire and is indeed an outstanding example. Many people have a 'flutter' on the football pools, and eagerly check the match results on Saturday, to find again that although the forecast was very near, it was just not good enough. It is the same with trying to raise a new carnation. The odds are about equal.

Taking Cuttings
Vegetative reproduction by propagating side shoots or 'cuttings' reproduces in the main the same characteristics, vigour, etc, as the stem from which the cutting is taken. Needless to say, then, it is vital to take the utmost care in selecting the plant and indeed the stem from which to take your cuttings.

A well-grown carnation will have a stem varying from 45 to 90 cm in length. Each stem will have approximately 12 nodes, or pairs of leaves. Each such node will produce one side shoot which, nearer the top, will be more or less only side buds. These are normally taken off (disbudded), before the main bud attains any size in order to improve the size and form of the ultimate bloom. The very lowest 'breaks' or side shoots are usually very contracted and stubby. These will not be very good cuttings to use as propagating material, for they will produce plants which are very slow and usually produce blooms of very inferior quality. Furthermore, the plant produced from this type of cutting will be more susceptible to disease.

A typical carnation 'stock house', where carnation plants are grown specifically for the production of cuttings. Checking and roguing are carried out at frequent intervals, and only selected workers are permitted to enter such houses. Cuttings are being chosen here for propagation.

There is of course a good deal of difference between the methods adopted by commercial growers and those which the amateur will follow. It always will be so and is unavoidable. The large commercial grower will have special plants grown for 'stock'; such plants are from special, selected clone stocks and undergo frequent selecting and roguing during the whole season before the propagating period arrives.

All cuttings intended to provide the plants for the mother stock department first of all pass through the laboratory for 'culturing', which means that each cutting is individually tested for disease within the plant tissue so that it is possible to make absolutely certain that only disease-free material is propagated, which for the entire period of the subsequent two years is grown under conditions of complete isolation. The utmost care is taken to see that there is no likelihood of them becoming infected during the subsequent growing period.

This, of course, is only possible where large quantities are grown and propagated each year. For the amateur grower it is not necessary in any way, provided he maintains a healthy stock and only adds to his collection new cultivars and plants obtained from a source of supply which guarantees such plants to be free from vascular disease. In the case of the amateur who normally grows his plants in pots, risk of the spread of disease from one plant to another is lessened, in any case, by the fact that the root system of each plant is confined to the pot in which the plant grows.

It is obvious, too, that an amateur grower could not grow stock plants in the same way as the larger commercial grower, for such stock plants are only allowed to produce one or, at the most, two flowers, and all other shoots are 'stopped' throughout the season in order to produce the best type of cuttings. Bearing in mind that the amateur grows all his plants for the flowers they will produce, I would suggest that to compromise only one, the most vigorous shoot of each plant that one wishes to reproduce, is stopped by the end of the summer at the very latest, when four to six good cuttings may be taken during mid- and late winter.

Such cuttings when taken are removed with a downward-backward pull in such a manner that the 'heel', or that portion of the base of the shoot which is attached to the main stem, is taken off intact.

When a flower stem has been cut back as suggested above, the flower stem which has elongated to form a bud is pinched off at a point above which worthless bud shoots (side buds) are formed. This is usually at the fifth or sixth node below the main bud (*see* Fig. 10).

If unrooted cuttings are obtained from a commercial plant nursery, it may well be that such cuttings do not show a 'heel' when received. This, however, is no cause for alarm, but is due to a special technique practised by the commercial establishment to save labour, and invariably on a nursery where the use of knives has long been abolished. The reason for this is explained in the chapter on pests and diseases. The fact that such a cutting is broken out instead of pulled off by the 'heel' does not mean that it is a 'top' cutting and therefore undesirable. A top cutting is the tip of a stem which has elongated to form a bud. If the shoot has reached a length of more than 20 cm before it is taken as a cutting then it would generally constitute a 'top' cutting and in such a case would seldom make a desirable plant. Such cuttings are distinguished by the length of stem between the nodes and the leaf formation at the tip, and are easily recognised by an experienced grower. Such cuttings would never be sent out by a firm of repute to fulfil orders for rooted cuttings, even if supplies were short.

With such cultivars as the 'Sims', which are now very numerous and widely grown, coupled with the fact that due to the many desirable characteristics of 'Sim' cultivars, raisers and breeders use these as 'parents' in their breeding programme, and when one remembers that all 'Sims' have a tall habit and consequently tend to pass this on to their offspring, cuttings from such cultivars will have more length of stem between nodes than the dwarfer and more compact cultivars. This, therefore, should not be confused when cuttings are taken or have been purchased.

Cuttings should be taken only from clean, healthy and vigorous plants. Failure to observe this fundamental rule will cause a cultivar to deteriorate, will lower production, produce flowers of lesser quality and substance, render the ultimate stock less resistant to disease, and eventually result in a stock which in no way compares with the original.

It should be remembered that most carnation diseases, with the possible exception of rhizoctonia stem rot, may be carried in the cuttings. Therefore no plant which shows any signs or any trace or possibility of disease, or which is located close to diseased plants, should be used to provide propagating material.

A danger which occurs too often is that cuttings are taken off the flower stem after the stems have been cut, either in the nursery grading room or, as in the case of the amateur grower, when they have been taken into the house, and it is found that a few cuttings are left on the stem. Do not use such cuttings for propagation as it is impossible to know what type of plant they came from or what its environment was and there would always be the danger of propagating from a weak or undesirable plant.

A good deal has often been said about 'over-propagation'. This, to say the least, is a misleading and over-rated term. It depends on what is implied by over-propagation. Actually there is no such thing, as over-propagation is nothing short of careless propagation, and I would interpret this expression to mean to

41

Examples of good and bad cuttings. The two on the right are the type we would select for propagation; the one on the left would be discarded as it has elongated too much (note space between each pair of leaves).

42

propagate all and every shoot which can be taken from a plant. It may well be that a fairly bushy plant has no satisfactory cuttings at all and therefore even one top shoot taken from such a plant could be called 'over-propagation'; whereas a commercial and well-grown stock plant could produce as many as 40 or 60 very good cuttings, and if all such cuttings were used for propagation I would consider that 'over-propagation' was the case.

The following practices are also careless or over-propagation: propagation from diseased or weak stock; taking thin, elongated shoots from the upper part of the stems; taking short squatty shoots from the hard wood at the base of the stem; taking cuttings that are too small, or top cuttings from shoots that have run up to form bud.

The Propagating Season

The propagating season extends from mid-autumn until the middle of spring, although commercial growers, especially those who specialise in offering rooted cuttings and plants for sale, often start in early autumn and not infrequently propagate in late spring in order to meet the demand for cuttings for very early or late planting. Generally speaking, carnation cuttings can be rooted, provided appropriate facilities are available, throughout the 12 months of the year. Mid-winter to early spring, however, will always be considered to be the most desirable period for propagation of carnation cuttings. This, in particular, I would suggest for the amateur grower.

The cultivars which grow slowly are best propagated early, whereas those cultivars which are more rapid would be better left until late winter or early spring.

Preparing Cuttings

The quicker cuttings are 'prepared' and inserted after they have been taken the better. It would be wrong to leave cuttings to wilt, and if for some reason or other cuttings cannot be handled very soon after they have been taken from the plant, it is best to put them in a polythene bag which should be closed at the top and kept in as cool a place as possible.

Properly handled, cuttings can be kept for a fairly long period, and, in fact, this is a practice which is followed on a few of the

43

most up-to-date commercial nurseries. By means of refrigeration, cuttings can be kept for eight or nine months quite satisfactorily. I should warn the ambitious and experimentally-minded amateur, however, that the ordinary domestic 'fridge' will not serve the purpose. The temperature in such a small refrigerator will not be maintained accurately enough. The temperature variation for the suitable storage of cuttings is very critical and should not exceed 1°C (33°F) or fall below 0°C (32°F). Furthermore, the temperature in a domestic appliance varies between the top and the bottom, besides which, the more frequent opening of the door causes fluctuations which will be detrimental to the cuttings.

The type of refrigerator used by commercial growers varies from 11 to 42 m³ capacity and has, as well as refrigeration, a small heating plant installed. The latter comes into operation directly the temperature drops below 0°C (32°F) when at the same time the cooling motor is switched off. When the temperature rises to above 0°C (32°F) the heater is cut out and when 1°C (33°F) is reached the cooling element motor cuts in and so on. In addition to such installation, we have small low volume fans fitted, at least three for a 11 m³ cold box and more or larger fans for the larger cool room, which are essential to maintain not only air movement but also to ensure that one part of the refrigerator is not cooler or warmer than the other.

Although such refrigeration and storage of cuttings is not a practice which will be adopted or indeed required by the amateur carnation grower, the above brief explanation might be useful, especially as more and more up-to-date methods are brought into use in the commercial field and one frequently hears about 'refrigerated', 'cultured', 'heat-treated' cuttings and so on.

It has for a long time been a wise practice to treat the cuttings before preparation with a fungicide and maybe also an insecticide, before they are placed in the propagating bin or frame. This may be done immediately they are removed from the plants. It is better to do this before they have been prepared. The treatment consists of immersing the cuttings in a solution containing fungicide and insecticide, which must be chemically compatible, and water added according to manufacturer's directions. I hesitate to prescribe any particular fungicide or insecticide for

44

this purpose; new chemicals are being constantly brought on to the markets and I am sure that whatever I recommend at the time these notes are being written will be superseded by new materials five years from now. I will, therefore, confine my suggestion to what is our practice to date in 1981. We use a zineb base fungicide in combination with TEPP insecticide but as the latter is only available to the commercial grower we would recommend the following only for commercial use.

92 g zineb (the Murphy Chemical Co. Ltd.), and 11 cc TEPP to 45 l. water.

For the amateur 28 cc Lindex in 9 l. of water (2 standard teaspoons in 2.2 l. with one sachet Orthocide captan fungicide in 2.2 l.) is suggested. The cuttings should be dipped long enough to wet them. Lindex, however, would only be effective against aphids or thrips on the cuttings. If there is a possibility of red spider mite infestation also to be eliminated Lindex should be replaced by Murphy's Systemic Insecticide at the same rate of 28 cc per 9 l., to which Orthocide captan is added as already recommended.

Both Lindex and Murphy's Systemic Insecticide are compatible with Orthocide captan.

Cuttings should never be placed in clear water before insertion, even if by so doing one is apt to think that they become more crisp and therefore would be the better for this drink. Such a practice would be the most certain invitation to the spread of disease from perhaps only one unexpected but disease-infected cutting.

If the cuttings were taken from the plants with the 'heel' intact, a sharp but clean knife should be used to make a cut directly below one of the lower nodes. The two leaves immediately above the cut are removed and no further trimming should be done. The more up-to-dateyway, however, would be to break the cutting at one of the nodes, where a reasonably clean break can be made.

I would at all times recommend disposing of the knives altogether, except for the use of cutting raffia or string for tying the plants, or sharpening the pencil to make certain that the name of the cultivar is clearly written on the label. It has been proved beyond doubt that where spread of disease was rapid, as well as frequent, it was mainly the knife which was the cause. Discontinuation of its use in the preparation of cuttings, picking of the flowers, etc, showed a remarkable and unmistakable improvement.

Once the art of breaking at the joint has been mastered, and I am sure it will present some difficulty at first, it will later be as easy as cutting with a knife. As before, only the two leaves directly above the break should be removed by pulling off, but only if they are likely to interfere with inserting the cuttings in the sand. So after breaking at the node do not take any more leaves off, i.e. make any more 'wounds', if it can be avoided. Remember that any such 'wound' made is another possible point of fungal infection.

It may be that some of my readers, even after patient practice, will still have difficulty in making a proper break, and the only thing then is to go back to the knife. If there should be a possibility of disease, due to the recent loss of a few plants, I would suggest having a small jar of methylated spirits and a lighted candle, so that after each cut is made the knife can be dipped into the spirit and flamed over the candle, which should destroy any disease organism present on the knife blade. If this is a practical proposition, then there is no objection to the use of a knife.

Frequently, I have been asked as to the virtue or otherwise of the use of rooting hormones. I know there are growers who use these regularly and with excellent results, but I do not use hormones for rooting unless absolutely necessary. If cuttings do not root, it is not always due to lack of hormones; it could be lack of bottom heat, lack of moisture or an incorrect propagating medium, such as sand which is too fine or sand which contains too much stone and is therefore too open.

There are a few cultivars which even with proper facilities are difficult, and, in such cases, I would certainly recommend the use of a powder hormone. I would never use a hormone liquid and place cuttings prepared for insertion into an inch or so of such solution for one or two hours. As mentioned before it is a definite invitation to the spread of disease and must be avoided. The use of hormone powder is safe. After preparing the cuttings, dip them about 13 mm in the powder and shake off any surplus; then they are ready for insertion.

A common cause for failure in rooted cuttings can be traced to cuttings taken while the plants themselves are dry at the roots. I suggest, therefore, that on the day before it is intended to gather cuttings all plants are given a thorough watering to overcome any possibility of failure, at least on this score.

Propagating Frames and Mist Propagation

Some form of propagating 'bin' or 'frame' is required. This can easily be made up by using a large-size wooden box some 22–25 cm deep. The bottom could be taken out completely and re-nailed with spaces between the boards to encourage free drainage. Alternatively, holes 2.5 cm in diameter could be drilled all over the bottom to answer the same purpose. Another way of making a box for propagating is to take out the bottom entirely and replace this with a few battens, halfway between the bottom and top of the box, on which are placed tiles—this is the best, for these will ensure all the drainage required as well as retaining moisture.

At each end of the box two uprights are nailed from one side to the other; lengthways a strong batten is fixed to form a ridge. Pieces of glass are set slanting from the sides to the ridge and the

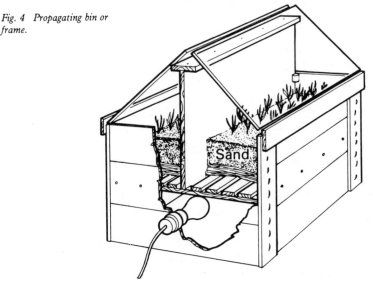

Fig. 4 Propagating bin or frame.

end can be closed off by glass cut at a suitable angle to ensure complete enclosure of the frame (*see* Fig. 4).

Somehow or other it is necessary to provide a little bottom heat underneath our propagating bin so as to maintain a constant temperature of 13°C (55°F) in the sand with which the bin will be partially filled.

If you have hot-water pipes in your greenhouse this should solve the difficulty, as the propagating bin can be placed directly over the pipes and closed in underneath to conserve the warmth. I have even heard of people maintaining the necessary temperature under a small propagating box by means of an electric light bulb. The best method of all would be an electric soil warmer, if an adequate number of cuttings are to be propagated. Advertisements in the gardening papers show that a great many of these heaters are now obtainable, and if in doubt ask your local electrical engineer for advice.

It is not the purpose of this book to recommend one or other manufacturer, but a look at the many advertisements will show that there are a number of very sophisticated propagating frames available with a proviso for base heating and temperature control, some even with a complete mist installation. The expense may be somewhat unwarranted, as the propagating frame illustrated in Fig. 4 gives excellent results and is inexpensive and simple.

The bottom of the bin, whether wood or tiles, is covered with a thin layer of coarse but clean ashes or broken-up clinker, but ensure at all times the utmost cleanliness.

If propagating in pans which take approximately 25–30 cuttings, the pans, after cuttings have been inserted, are placed on the ashes, but as I would prefer to propagate direct into the frame I would fill the bin with some really clean-washed, sharp sand to a depth of 7–10 cm. Water this sand well and firm it by means of a wooden rammer, i.e. a flat piece of wood with a handle. After firming, water once more and all should be set to commence inserting the cuttings.

There is, however, something to be said for propagating in pans. It is true that cuttings in pans can easily be taken from the frame, prior to potting, for hardening off, and this is an advantage. Nevertheless, more care needs to be paid to the watering, for it can easily be overdone. Sand in a bin maintains the moisture longer than sand in shallow pans. You could, however, place the pans on a layer of ashes in the propagating bin, but these minor details are determined by different conditions. Propagating pans are usually some 15–17 cm in diameter and 7.5–9 cm in depth. They are provided either with a large drainhole in the centre of the bottom, or three smaller ones at the sides. The hole or holes are covered with a good crock and are then filled with clean-washed sharp sand. Always make certain the sand is perfectly clean. If in doubt, a thorough washing is advised. The pans are filled to within 13 mm of the rim and well watered in. After being left to drain from half an hour to one hour, they are ready for insertion of the cuttings.

When it has been decided not to use pans but to propagate direct into the bin, sand is placed on the ash or clinker covered bottom to a depth of 7–10 cm, which is quite sufficient. This also should receive a thorough watering, and after firming with a piece of flat wood, cuttings may be inserted.

From my experience, I do not think one need firm the sand too much, provided always a sharp sand is used of not too fine a texture. Very fine sand such as preferred by a bricklayer for building purposes would not be suitable.

The Big Top propagator. Plenty of headroom is available for growing on young plants as well as for rooting cuttings. The base is glass-fibre, with an aluminium-framed glazed top.

49

Vermiculite has been recommended as an alternative to sharp sand and many claims have been made for this material. It is true that carnation cuttings root well in Vermiculite. The reason for this is not the material as such but the fact that moisture is held longer and, more importantly, air and consequently more oxygen is available more freely, hence more efficient rooting. It is my experience, however, that moisture is held too well, and over the years I have found that cuttings rooted in Vermiculite were more prone to damping off or later in life were more susceptible to stem rot diseases. One may often notice that cuttings rooted in Vermiculite have a much enlarged base from which the rootlets emerge, and it is, moreover, much larger than it was when the cutting was inserted. I feel that this enlarging could well be responsible for the susceptibility to stem diseases at a later stage and because of this I do not use or recommend Vermiculite.

Highly recommended, however, is Perlite. This is a volcanic material which, after having been subjected to very high temperatures, is crushed and forms the ideal material for propagating purposes. It is inert, that is to say there is no chemical reaction; it is stable, meaning it is always the same, which one cannot always say for sand, even if it comes from the same pit. It is extremely light and can be used over and over again. Drainage is perfect, yet it holds water well, and aeration is excellent. It is best if it is mixed with a good horticultural medium grade peat. A mixture of 2 parts Perlite and 1 part granulated horticultural peat is to be recommended.

For those who use such a mixture for propagation of cuttings during the summer period I would suggest that they use peat and Perlite in equal parts.

For those who take the matter really seriously and wish to emulate the commercial practice so as to attain similar standards of success, and do not mind some initial expense, in order to achieve their aim and be up to date, I must mention the mist propagation unit.

Mist propagation is now practised by all commercial growers. Commercially one could not exist without mist propagation facilities, apart from the fact that this technique also produces superior plants.

The advantages are many, but the initial cost will be the

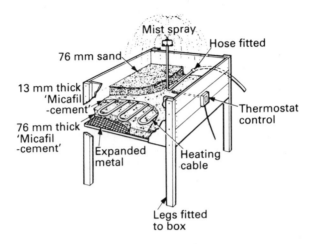

Fig. 5 *A single mist propagation unit.*

deciding factor as far as the amateur is concerned. In making such a decision it would be right to say that not only do the carnation cuttings benefit from such a facility, but one could with great advantage also use the unit for all sorts of cuttings such as chrysanthemums, pelargoniums and so on, and cuttings of otherwise difficult subjects such as hydrangeas, magnolia and camellia, as well as species of conifers, would prove to be fairly simple.

Many amateur units have been in use for many years, and propagation by the amateur has consequently been made much easier, and an almost 100 per cent certainty of striking is ensured. There are, of course, various types available from various manufacturers. The installations at our nurseries have given many years of reliable and trouble-free service, and on those grounds we would be happy to recommend to all concerned the mist units, large or small, manufactured under the name of MacPenny's Mist Propagation, Gore Road, New Milton, Hampshire, England.

It consists of a 'unit' solenoid valve with filter and an electronic leaf, if the latter is the correct name, for it does not in any way represent a leaf as we know it, but is a small and specially designed control apparatus containing two electrodes which are connected by a film of moisture when placed amongst the cuttings, thus preventing the mist from being operated. Directly the moisture film is evaporated the contact between the two electrodes is broken and causes the operation of the solenoid valve which is connected to the ordinary mains supply, and a very fine, mist-like spray is emitted from the specially designed nozzles.

Each nozzle will cover an area of 1.5 m in diameter. It would of course be difficult to make a circular propagating frame for the smallest unit. The best way would be to prepare a suitable frame, say 0.6 m square, with the one misting nozzle placed in the centre.

The better idea, if sufficient use could be made of the available space, would be a propagating bench, 1 m wide and 1.7 m long, which would be adequately served by two nozzles, each one being positioned 40 cm from each end, leaving a distance of 85 cm between the nozzles. It should be remembered that the greater part of the cost is in the 'unit' and the 'solenoid valve', the price of each nozzle being only small in comparison. It is, therefore, as well to make the propagating area large enough.

To complete this 'set-up' I would make a special base to the bench or frame and incorporate a mains-operated heating cable to dispense with a costly transformer. This base must have perfect drainage and is best made by using a mixture of 4 parts Micafil, obtainable from builders' merchants and intended for use as an insulating material, to 1 part of cement. Water is added and a thorough but not too wet a mix should be the aim. A preliminary base made of a few laths covered with a thin old sack would be an ideal base on which to place this mixture. It should be lightly levelled off and not rammed or consolidated, otherwise the porosity of the base will be impaired. The first layer should be approximately 75 mm thick and will set by the next day.

The heating cable is laid out on this. (I must give a word of warning here and recommend you to consult your local Electricity Board, where free advice can be obtained as to the length of cable needed according to the temperature required; also, full technical details may be obtained from this source.)

The next operation is to place a 25-mm layer of rendering of

Mist propagation can be used by the amateur as well as the commercial carnation grower for propagating by means of cuttings and also for raising seed.

the foregoing Micafil/cement mixture over the cable. The surface is trowelled backwards and forwards without undue pressure on the trowel so as to give a smooth surface on which afterwards you can use a shovel for removal of sand. This surface will be quite hard and firm and yet will drain as freely as a sieve.

Only 5 cm or at the most a depth of 6 cm sand or other propagating medium is required.

Thus the temperature as well as watering and hand syringing is taken care of. The latter is looked after by the electronic leaf already mentioned, and the base temperature by means of a rod-type thermostat which is placed horizontally about 13 mm above the permanent base of the bin, and extending from the side for its entire length (usually some 45 cm) into the sand.

For ordinary propagation, a temperature of 15–16°C (58–60°F) is required, but where the 'mist unit' is in use my recommendation would be a 5°C (10°F) increase. The ambient or air temperature of the house in both cases should not be higher than 11–13°C (52–55°F). Especially under mist, ventilation should be given freely when conditions permit and the overhead air temperature should not be allowed to increase without opening the ventilators.

After 2–2½ weeks, cuttings under 'mist' will be making roots and mist should be operated by hand. We call this the process of 'weaning', i.e. the number of 'bursts' of mist are determined and the system is manually operated by means of a switch. It depends, of course, on weather conditions at the time. If the day when 'weaning' is to commence is dull, and 'dew' on the plants is fairly heavy, all that will be required is one or two bursts during midday or afternoon. During a sunny day the number of bursts is increased accordingly.

The next day the number is reduced, and unless the third day is extremely sunny and warm no mist will be needed. It is obvious, too, that at that time the temperature in the sand can be reduced, and the thermostat setting lowered to maintain a steady 16°C (60°F).

By the end of the third week or certainly by the beginning of the fourth week the cuttings are ready for potting.

There are some who would prefer to use propagating pans, whereas others would rather propagate direct into the frame. Insertion in this form can be made easier if a piece of flatboard the size of the pan is used, with a handle on the upper part; nails which protrude through the board approximately 25–38 mm are driven through it and are spaced so that a 15 cm pan accommodates approximately 25 cuttings. Press this board into the sand, which has been watered thoroughly, and the position for each cutting will be clearly marked after the nail-board has been withdrawn. The small holes left will prevent damage to the base of the cuttings caused by insertion into the sharp gritty sand.

A similar device can easily be made for cuttings to be inserted direct into the propagating medium placed in the propagating frame or on to the propagating bench. The size of the board will depend on the size of bin or bench width.

A piece of board, preferably oak, say 22–25 cm in width, and either the full width of the bench, or for really wide benches, half the width, and about 2.5 cm thick, would be best. Again 6-cm nails driven through the board, protruding 2.5–4 cm, with the point downwards, in straight rows and about 2.5 cm apart, with the rows of nails about 5 cm apart, would be the ideal tool for marking the positions where the cuttings are to be inserted.

Aftercare
When cuttings have been inserted, whether the mist propagating unit or a simply devised propagating frame is used, a thorough watering immediately afterwards is essential.

Shading may also be necessary during bright spells to avoid unnecessary transpiration by cuttings which cannot replenish their moisture requirements until roots have formed, but overshading must be avoided. During the first week or ten days it may be necessary to syringe the cuttings with a fine hand syringe to avoid wilting, but this too should not be overdone. Obviously there would be more need of this in prolonged bright weather than during a period of dull and humid conditions.

Watering should be attended to. It is impossible to lay down any definite ruling on this for it depends on how quickly the sand or other propagating medium will dry out. Keep it reasonably moist at all times and, on average, the watering can would be needed once a week while the frame is closed, but directly ventilation is given the process of drying will be hastened. However, this is only a guide, and observation is necessary in order to determine when or when not to water cuttings.

At the best of times there will be occasions when cuttings do not 'strike' as well, or at all, as might be expected even when everything seems to have been provided to ensure good results. There are certain cultivars which always cause difficulty and these are usually referred to as 'difficult strikers'. As mentioned earlier, hormone powder will often give better results. Another cause or reason for bad rooting or total failure would be that cuttings were taken from plants which were too dry at the root. This must always be avoided, and if in doubt it is as well to give the plant to be propagated from a good watering the day before taking cuttings.

A further word on the propagating medium would not be amiss. Sand can vary a great deal and I have experienced unbelievable disappointments with different deliveries of sand which came from the same pit. Although one seam may be perfect for our purpose, the next seam may be totally unsuitable.

After the first week a little air could be admitted to the frame by placing a piece of wood under the glass against the ridge, while shading could be dispensed with, except during extremely bright weather. Bottom heat, i.e. a temperature of 10°C (50°F), should be our aim. Always keep the overhead temperature at 2–5°C (5–10°F) below the actual sand temperature.

During the second week after the insertion of the cuttings it will be necessary to see if the medium on the bench or in the propagating bench requires watering, that is of course if mist propagation is not used, but be careful not to water unless really necessary. At no time should the base of the cuttings be permitted to become dry; at the same time over-watering or watering *ad lib* must be avoided.

It is impossible to enlarge further on this question of watering, as propagation, weather and environmental conditions vary so widely and can often change two or three times each week. It depends, too, on the amount of bottom heat one has to provide to maintain the required temperature in the medium, as to how soon or how frequently the medium will dry out to warrant further watering. Watering, not only during the propagating stages, but throughout the growth of the plant, will always remain one of the real arts of growing plants, and this has to be learned by careful observation, the application of common sense, and trial and error.

If a mist propagating unit is used, the grower has no further worries in regard to watering once the cuttings have been watered in immediately after insertion, from that time until the cuttings are lifted. Nor is there any need to shade the cuttings placed under mist.

Shading for the first 10 days is essential, however, for cuttings propagated in a propagating frame or bin without mist, more so of course during periods of bright sunshine, in order to prevent excessive transpiration. For the same reason and to achieve the same end, hand syringing the cuttings within the enclosed propagating frame is essential once or maybe twice a day, according to weather conditions, in order to maintain a humid atmosphere around the cuttings.

By the same token, cuttings under mist can be subjected to normal ventilation because the more rapidly the cutting foliage dries the more quickly the electronic leaf will dry and cause the misting to be operated more frequently, thus maintaining the humidity which prevents excessive transpiration.

In regard to cuttings in the propagating frame not enjoying the benefits of mist, it may be necessary during the second week after insertion to consider whether shading can be dispensed with. This will of course depend on prevailing weather conditions. It may also be necessary to admit a little ventilation to the frame. In the case of my own 'home-made' propagating frame this can easily be done by placing a small piece of wood or an empty matchbox between the upper edge of the glass and the ridge bar. Once we start to ventilate and the cuttings begin to root, ventilation of the frame can become a daily routine.

All the time we endeavour to maintain a temperature in the propagating medium of around 13–15°C (55–58°F), for mist-propagated cuttings a few degrees higher, and an overhead temperature from 2–5°C (5–10°F) below the temperature at the base of the cuttings.

Fourteen days after insertion the glass could be removed altogether and shading should not be necessary now unless the plants show embarrassment during bright periods. The moisture content of the sand is very important. More ventilation can be given to the greenhouse itself, if weather conditions are favourable, and in the third week we should begin to harden off the cuttings in readiness for removal from the frame for potting up during the fourth week.

As soon as the cuttings are sufficiently rooted, it is important to remove them from the sand without unnecessary delay and to see about potting-up into small pots.

Remember that while the cuttings are in the sand they cannot find any nutrition on which to sustain new growth, and should they grow at all when still in the sand this will only be on air and water plus bottom heat, and will result in weak growth instead of that sturdiness which we are looking for in young carnation plants.

It can happen with the amateur propagator, as it does from time to time with the commercial propagator, that for some reason or other cuttings ready for lifting cannot be attended to and have to be held on the benches. Apart from lifting at the appropriate time and the placing of cuttings in the cold store, which does not cause deterioration in any way, provided storage is not prolonged and an accurate temperature can be maintained, there is nothing else we can do but to take care of cuttings by liquid feeding while being held on the bench. An excellent feed for such a purpose would be: 680 g potassium nitrate and 170 g ammonium nitrate dissolved in 4.5 l warm water, which for use is diluted with more water at the rate of 1:200 parts.

Even so, it should not be considered if one can avoid this treatment and should only be applied in an emergency. It would be far better to find the time to lift and pot or plant the cuttings at the correct time.

On average, and provided the proper facilities exist throughout the period of rooting, it should take about four weeks to root the cuttings (i.e. four weeks after insertion of the cutting is should be ready for lifting and subsequent treatment—potting-on or planting out).

It should be clear by now that cuttings in the propagating frame, without mist, would by the beginning of the fourth week be standing in the frame without the glass covering and certainly without shading. The base temperature could be reduced as a form of weaning, by 2°C (5°F) or so.

Likewise the cuttings under mist must be weaned during the last week or 10 days prior to lifting. First of all, the frequency of the mist is reduced either by hand operation or by a weaning device which is obtainable from the manufacturer. Here, too, the bench or media temperature is gradually reduced so that for some days immediately before lifting the temperature reading would be nearer 9°C (48°F).

Multipots

A point I have not mentioned in my references to propagation is the use of multipots.

A multipot tray is a moulded plastic tray approximately 53 cm long and 30 cm wide, into which are moulded rows of small pots, all in one piece. There are trays of large and small pots, and the number of such pots per tray depends obviously on the size of the pot mould.

For propagating carnations we have over the last four or five years had outstanding success by using the 33 mm diameter pot-hole which has a 38 mm depth. Each tray was eight rows of 12 such pots per row. A complete tray accommodates, therefore, 96 cuttings, each completely separated from the other. In the bottom of each pot-hole is a small hole for drainage.

Carnation cuttings rooted in Perlite and peat in a multipot tray. Such cuttings are superior to bench- or pan-propagated cuttings as, upon lifting out of the tray, there is no root disturbance, and once planted or potted such cuttings will grow away more rapidly.

The use of such trays has many advantages. First of all, there is considerable economy in the Perlite/peat mixture. Another advantage is that 96 cuttings can be handled at the same time. It makes it easier, too, for weaning if during that process it necessitates moving the almost rooted cuttings into a different environment out and away from the actual propagating bench. Commercially, too, it has untold advantages. When planting out is upon us, complete trays can be taken from the propagating department, after a thorough watering, which must not be omitted, and taken to the house or beds to be planted. The trays can be placed on the bed or part thereof where the variety will be planted, sometimes a day or more before planting actually begins.

Provided the rootballs or the medium are not allowed to dry out, the rooted cuttings can stand there unplanted for a day or two without coming to any harm.

It is much easier, too, with multipot cuttings, to avoid deep planting, which is so important with carnations, for one can see the surface of the soil ball, and therefore can keep this level with the surrounding bed soil when planting. What, to my mind, is the greatest advantage of all, whether to the amateur or commercial grower, is the fact that there is no root disturbance or root damage. If, just before planting, each tray is thoroughly watered, each small rootball will come out of the mould quite easily and cleanly by a gentle pull upwards. The soil ball is completely intact and no root whatsoever is lost or damaged. It is for this reason, I believe, that such multipot rooted cuttings can be planted even in summer during bright sunny weather without any fear of wilting, and the obvious result is a plant which becomes more rapidly established, consequently produces breaks better and more freely because such plants do not experience any check, and ultimately, therefore, produce an earlier and better crop.

With reasonable care these multipot trays can last several years, in fact we have such trays which have been in regular use for four or more years. After lifting each batch, the trays are collected and before further use are chemically sterilised. A word of warning: do not steam sterilise such plastic trays—they are not suitable for this form of sterilising.

Potting to Planting Out

The lifting of the cuttings from the bin, or pans, should be done with care. With much care and attention young rootlets have been produced on bare cuttings. This has taken four weeks, or thereabouts, to accomplish, and it would be folly to remove the cuttings in a careless manner so that many of these tender roots are damaged or entirely broken off.

Do not remove too many from the propagating medium at the same time so that they lie about for a considerable time before being placed in the small pot. Should the roots be somewhat dry, dip them in some clean water before potting them into the new soil. Never pot, plant, or re-pot a plant which is dry at the roots.

Types of Pots
The first type of pot is the conventional clay pots which have been used for many years and there is nothing to be said against them. It is essential, however, that they are perfectly clean if plants have been grown in them before. The best procedure would be to scrub them and if possible to steam sterilise them afterwards. This would make certain that the new plants to be potted could not become affected by any disease which may lie dormant in the pot. The pot should also be dry, for potting into damp or moist pots will later present difficulties when the soil ball has to be knocked out for either re-potting or planting.

I should mention, too, that if new clay pots have to be purchased it would be unwise to use them without a thorough soaking. New clay pots will absorb an enormous amount of water. Unless they are treated, as follows, and used for potting young plants, one will find that they dry out rapidly because the pots will absorb the moisture applied to the soil. When bringing pots home after purchase or after taking delivery it is best to soak the entire quantity in a bucket, tank or barrel full of water, covering all pots, and leaving to soak for a day or even two days. Thereafter, stack the pots in a neat stack and allow them to dry because, as already mentioned, the inner pot wall must be dry before we use the pots for actually potting the young plants.

All this is obviously obviated if plastic pots are used. However, I am sufficiently old fashioned to have an inclination towards the clay pot in preference to plastic. The plastic pot has its uses, even for carnations, but in my opinion only if used as a short-term container. The plastic 5 cm pot would therefore be acceptable but I would not use 15 or 22 cm pot in plastic as a container for a carnation plant for a period of 12 months or more, at least not for amateur purposes.

If plastic pots are used, the experienced grower would find that far less watering is needed, as the soil in the plastic pot does not dry out as rapidly as the soil in a clay pot. You might think that is excellent, as there will be less work to do. I feel, however, that there is something lost in aeration of the soil in a plastic pot as opposed to the porous clay pot, and this to my mind is an important point.

My advice to anyone used to growing plants in clay pots and for some reason changing over to plastic pots is to watch the watering carefully. Do not overdo it, and try and learn by observation how frequently the plants should be watered. This can only be ascertained by knocking a plant here and there out of the pot and examining the moisture content of the lower part of the soil ball. Although the upper part may show dryness, often one would find the lower part too moist to warrant the application of more water.

There are, however, a good many other types of pots which have made their appearance during recent years. There are the mulch paper pots, which I consider unsuitable, and I advise against their use for carnations. They invariably cause nitrogen starvation due to ammonia being absorbed during the decomposition process of the material of which these pots are manufactured, and although the plants at first appear to grow quite happily after some three or four weeks they will become starved and stunted due to lack of nitrogen.

I would not be too happy, either, in using bitumen-treated paper pots. They do not decompose as rapidly as one would imagine when they are potted-on or planted out, and consequently the roots become strangled.

More recently polypots, a type of non-porous plastic pot, have been introduced. I think they may have a future for certain types of plants, but at present they are still rather expensive. At the same time we are faced with storage problems and subsequently with washing and sterilising pots before further use can be made of them.

My preference would be the peat-wood pulp pot, one of which is known as the 'Jiffy' pot. They are now available from almost all garden sundry shops in small and large packs. The cost is reasonable and during their manufacture they are impregnated with plant nutrients whereby deficiencies are eliminated. The plants, and especially carnations, do extremely well in them, and for the first potting I would use the 57 mm size, although smaller as well as larger sizes are available.

About 14 days after potting it will be noticed that very fine rootlets are penetrating the pot wall and after four or five weeks the whole surface of the pot will be a mass of roots.

The makers of these pots claim that 'pot-and-all' may be potted on or planted out. From experience with carnations I would not, however, recommend this. We have found that if this is practised the roots will *not* freely root out into the new surrounding soil and consequently the plant will *not* produce the expected root system. We prefer to remove the upper part of the peat fibre pot wall of the 64 mm pot prior to potting-on or planting out. The root damage so caused does not appear to have any effect on the future performance of the plant, but we do ensure that new roots grow out freely and quickly.

Obviously any plant needing potting-on or planting out must, prior to removal from any pot, be thoroughly watered and this applies equally to a Jiffy pot-grown plant.

By using this type of pot the necessity of pot washing or sterilising is eliminated, because such a pot, unlike the clay or plastic pot, is never re-used.

Composts

If it is decided to use clay pots, which would be my next choice, I would use a 5 cm diameter pot for the first potting and a soil mixture consisting of a good fibrous loam with sufficient sharp sand or mortar rubble added to form an open mixture. After sifting through a 6 mm sieve, a light dusting of chalk lime and a little bonemeal of the finer grade is all that is needed for the first potting soil. No fertilisers, however good, should be added as this may damage the roots which are not accustomed to soil at all, having hitherto been only in sand. The aim at this stage is not a rapid growth of the plant, but more the type of healthy root formation on which the plant's future will depend. The latter is more rapid in a slightly hungry soil than in a very fertile soil mixture. The loam used should be sweet and clean. By clean I mean free from pests and disease organisms. For this reason, in our nurseries we steam-sterilise all our potting soils. Not only do we destroy insects which are always present in good turfy loam, especially wireworm and leatherjackets, but we also do away with weed seeds, and thus obtain a really clean soil.

As carnations do not normally take kindly to freshly steamed soil we sterilise well in advance of our requirements. Usually we commence this work at the end of the summer and do enough to last us for a considerable time. We turn the soil after sterilisation on several occasions and by the time we actually start preparing the first soil for potting, it has mellowed down nicely.

As an alternative to soil steaming, formaldehyde at 1:49 parts of water may be used, but it cannot be expected to rid the soil of weeds as is the case with steam.

A heap of soil which must have been sifted is heavily watered with the formaldehyde solution and covered over with sacks and a tarpaulin for approximately one week. When the covers are taken off, the heap should be turned at least twice each week for some four weeks. It is best not to contemplate using soil which has been treated with formaldehyde until eight weeks after treatment, and even then we must make certain that no formaldehyde fumes remain in the soil.

Steam-sterilising always will remain the most certain and efficient way. The larger nurseries have of course a steaming plant, but the average amateur will say at once 'how can I steam a small quantity of soil?' Perhaps you only need a barrowful for all the potting you have to do. Well, there are several ways and means to overcome this difficulty. There are several types of small sterilisers on the market. One, an electric machine, claimed to be very efficient, would, in my opinion, suit an amateur carnation grower with a collection of say 100-200 plants very well.

The electric soil steriliser which I have seen in use by an amateur and which impressed me most was the Humex Soil Steriliser, obtainable in three sizes. Model 1 is a dual-purpose machine which would answer the purpose of the grower with a small glasshouse. It is intended as a soil steriliser, but when not in use can be used as a heater (1,500 watts). A water tray is included to provide humidity if this is required. Model 2 is a 3,000 watts model, but otherwise similar in all respects, and Model 3 is of 1,500 watt capacity, and is an immersion element unit producing steam which percolates the soil.

Should one not wish to be troubled with sterilising and mixing of soil, there are of course sources of supply where a ready mixed, steam-sterilised and tested potting compost can be purchased. Such composts are prepared ready for use, steam-sterilised in three grades: No. 1 for the first potting of newly rooted cuttings into thumb pots; No. 2 for potting-on into 6 or 7.5 cm pots; and the final potting soil No. 3 for the final potting-on into 15 or 18 cm pots. Potting compost No. 3 could also be used satisfactorily for filling beds for planting out into final quarters. These are the John Innes composts.

Again a further word of warning. The term 'John Innes Compost' is sometimes abused, and compost that is offered to amateur gardeners by the name of J.I. potting compost is not always the mixture as recommended by the John Innes Institute after many years of experimental and research work in finding a reasonable soil mixture to suit most, or at least a wide range of, pot-grown plants.

To add to my dilemma is the fact that so much of this soil is offered in polythene bags. To my mind this is almost the worst container for bagging such soil compost. These bags, sealed in the way they are, are completely air tight and soil, being living matter, would not remain chemically unchanged if stored in such bags for any length of time.

Certainly, we use large polythene sacks for the despatch of our steam-sterilised carnation soil from our nurseries, but first of all no soil composts are bagged until actual despatch, and secondly our recommendations on the bags say clearly, 'Do not prolong storage in this sack.'

We have carried out extensive experimental work in order to find out the length of time the soil could remain in such poly-thene bags or sacks, but our findings were not conclusive. Under some conditions we found a complete chemical change after only 14 days, probably due to a fairly high moisture content of the soil at that time. Another sample which, prior to bagging, showed a pH of 7.0, was tested after 14 days in the enclosed sack and was found to have a pH of 6.1.

We have also found upsets in NPK (Nitrogen/Phosphate/Potash) after polythene bag storage of a three-week period, and soil which remained in the bag for six weeks was found to be definitely harmful to the plants.

Paper sacks would be much more acceptable for this purpose, but would not be so suitable for despatch by road or rail.

We are therefore left with the problem, and my advice is to purchase your soil and compost requirements from a source which is known to retain soil or compost for short periods only, and immediately it is delivered to empty it out into a container, box or even a clean hessian sack.

Nothing should be added to any of these soils at all, as this would upset the correct balance of ingredients so carefully worked out to suit all the requirements of the carnation plant.

These soil mixtures are the same as we use for our own potting, and we have used them for quite a number of years with proven success. They are regularly tested for their lime content, and the loam used is from some very old meadow or pasture land which is full of fibre.

Needless to say, it would be unwise to use the No. 3 mixture for the potting-on of cuttings just taken from sand. The same would apply if we used the No. 1 mixture for the final potting. Each mixture is prepared for each particular move and stage of growth.

I have already been asked: 'Could I not use No. 1 soil with the addition of some fertiliser for the final potting?' My answer is definitely no. The texture of the first soil would be too fine for a pot larger than 5 cm diameter. The No. 3 soil, for instance, is not sifted at all, but is shredded, leaving a much coarser texture.

First Potting

It is important to see that the pots to be used are perfectly clean
and dry. They certainly must be dry and should have been
brought into the greenhouse sometime beforehand. A wet pot
used at potting time will give a lot of trouble later on.

All potting of carnation plants should be done moderately
firmly. Care must be taken that at each removal, or potting-on, at
no time is the plant placed deeper than it was originally in the
sand for propagating. Deep potting will often lead to serious
trouble and may in some cases even be fatal.

Soil for potting should not be too dry, but sufficiently moist so
that when a handful of soil is squeezed together it will adhere in
that shape, but when disturbed it will easily crumble.

Actually, potting is simple. It goes without saying that a potting bench should have been prepared with a supply of clean
pots and soil beforehand. When attempting potting for the first
time, learn to do the job correctly from the very start. It may
seem awkward at first, but it will soon become a routine which
can be done with closed eyes. Practice makes perfect.

Handle the cuttings with the left hand, and the pots and soil
with the right. Thus, with the right hand, scoop the little pot half
full with soil and place on the bench in front of you, while with
the left you will have already taken a cutting which is then held
above the pot with the roots just in the pot. With the right hand
scoop up a handful of soil and fill in around the stem of the plant.
Taking care not to insert the plant too deep, gently press the soil
around the cutting with the thumb and first finger of each hand
and tap the pot once or twice sharply on the bench. This is all
there is to be done, and the plant is potted. A little more practice
and it will be an easy task.

As each plant is potted, place it in a shallow box or tray so that
it will not be necessary to walk about each time to set plants
down one at a time, but a whole batch will be taken together, or
at least as many as your tray will hold. Place the plants neatly in
rows on an ash-covered bench and water in when your day's
potting is completed.

The first watering should be done well, so that the entire soil
ball is completely moistened. The surplus water will drain away,
therefore do water generously. Shading needs to be given if the

67

weather is bright, and unless the weather outside is really warm keep the house closed for the first three or four days. The plants will soon become established and shading could then be omitted, while a little air on the lee-side of the house would be permissible. This is increased as time goes on when, after a week or two, the ventilators can be used quite freely. The temperature after the first three or four days should be approximately 7–10°C (45–50°F) at night. It would be unwise to force growth by maintaining a higher temperature; the plant would soon lose all its sturdiness and become weak and spindly.

After a fortnight 4–7°C (40–45°F) at night is all that is needed. From now on, grow your plants as hardy as possible, within reason of course, but certainly do not coddle them at any time.

Successive watering will be necessary, but great attention must be paid to this, as on no account must water be applied when it is not really needed by the plant, or when the soil is sufficiently moist.

Watering is one of the most difficult matters on which to give advice at the best of times, and it is certainly much more difficult, if not impossible to do so on paper. Continuous watering, when there is sufficient moisture in the soil, tends to foul the soil and make it sour. By an occasional drying out, we let air in between the soil particles where water was previously, and thus the soil is kept aerated and maintains the right sweetness so much loved by carnation plants.

For some days after potting, the soil in the small pots will not dry out as rapidly as it will do later when the soil ball is well filled with roots—then watering may have to be done quite freely. As soon as the ball is well covered with roots it will be time for potting-on into 9 cm pots.

Leaving the plants in the small pots when they are thoroughly rooted through will lead to an over-abundance of roots in such a confined space as a 5 cm pot, and we would then say that the plant is becoming 'potbound'. This should at all times be avoided as it spoils plants and results in hard growth and, later, insufficient breaks. Prepare everything for the second potting well in advance, and the day before actually doing this work water thoroughly the plants to be potted.

Subsequent Potting

Again, clean dry pots are essential, as well as the correct soil mixture. As a larger pot is used, this second potting soil is sifted through a coarser sieve (a 13 mm square mesh would be ideal for this purpose). As the young plants will have a nice healthy root system by now, they will begin to search for more nutrition and a slightly enriched soil has to be prepared to build up a strong and vigorous plant.

The main ingredients are again a nice fibrous loam; to every 6 parts of this, after it has been sifted, add 1 part of well-decayed horse manure, which is also sifted. Also, some burnt earth, mortar or brick rubble should be added. Sharp sand is also a good ingredient if the loam is of a heavy type, for this will ensure an open soil. A sprinkle of chalk lime and a good carnation base manure completes the mixture.

As for the first potting the soil mixture must be moist but not too wet.

The practice was always to pot rooted cuttings first into small pots as mentioned in the previous chapter. The next move was into the 9 cm pot and finally into 15 or 18 cm pots which were the 'finals'. It was considered essential to move the plants in stages from one pot to a larger size. This practice is still reasonably sound although for the more experienced grower not the best.

During the years since 1950 commercial growers have been forced to study the economic management of their nurseries more carefully. The rising cost of labour and other overheads have made them examine what was necessary and what could be dispensed with.

In regard to potting, on our nursery many experiments were made in order to see where labour and other costs of production could be saved, and small scale experiments were at first made with potting rooted cuttings direct into final or 15 cm pots, as well as planting out in their permanent beds where the plants were to flower. There were, of course, disadvantages such as heating a large commercial house for a comparatively small number of small plants in beds or in 15 cm pots. It caused difficulties with watering as well, for it obviously took some time before such small plants made enough root to occupy such a large volume of soil. Watering had to be done very carefully and whether in the greenhouse, border, bed or final pot, frequently the plant had to be 'ball-watered' only, to maintain moisture around the roots without unduly moistening the entire soil. Soil not occupied by plant roots would become 'sour' if watered continually, and after a time would be unsuitable for plant growth.

This method, therefore, calls for a good deal of experience, but if it can be managed well it is certainly worthwhile. There is no further check to the plant by repeated re-potting. Once the plant is established it should not experience any further setback and consequently after the plant has been given its first 'stop' a larger number of breaks will be obtained than from those plants which have been given the various moves from one pot to another. I must mention again, however, that it calls for a good deal of common sense.

A somewhat easier procedure would be to pot the rooted cuttings first into the 5 cm clay or 7 cm Jiffy pot, and when rooted through well, to move them into the 15 or 18 cm pot, so dispensing with the intermediate 9 cm pot.

Whether the latter or the previous method is adopted, great care is necessary with watering. It must be borne in mind that the smaller the plant the less transpiration of moisture takes place and consequently less water is absorbed by the roots. Furthermore, young plants will not be encouraged to produce new roots in an over-moist soil.

Cuttings inserted in the sand as unrooted cuttings by the middle of January will be potted into 5 or 6.5 cm pots by about the middle of February (four or five weeks after insertion), and by the end of March should be ready for potting-on into 9 cm pots. By knocking a few plants out of the pots it will be seen, by the amount of fibrous roots around the soil ball, if potting-on is necessary.

Everything, such as potting bench, pots, etc, should be ready, as well as a suitable place on which to stand the pots afterwards. The plants themselves should be thoroughly watered at least an hour or so before potting, so that the entire ball is quite moist.

Partly fill the 9 cm pot with soil so that when the 5 cm soil ball is placed in the pot the surface is just below the rim of the 9 cm pot. Hold the plant with the left hand and fill in with new soil with the right. The thumb of each hand holding the pot is placed at the side of the plant, then without exerting any direct pressure on to the soil, the pot is tapped smartly on the bench to firm the soil around the ball. Perhaps a little more soil will be needed in the pot, and that is all. Do not fill the pot too full, however, and see to it that the old 5 cm ball is not covered more than is unavoidable.

Place the pots again on an ash- or shingle-covered bench, and water well in. The plants will not require any further attention until they become sufficiently dry to warrant a further watering. No shading will be necessary this time, and ventilation should be given quite freely.

The final potting into 15 or 18 cm pots is done before the roots become too excessive in the 9 cm pots, as this again would lead to undue hardening of the plants, with the consequent result that very few breaks are obtained after 'stopping' and such plants would therefore be useless, or at any rate inferior samples. When nicely covered with roots all over the 9 cm soil ball, they should be potted-on into the final pots.

These being pots in which the plants will flower and remain until the following year, it is natural that the soil mixture should contain sufficient fertility to last quite some time.

Only the best possible loam with a good percentage of fibre should be used. A good horticultural peat, well-decayed farmyard manure (horse-manure for a special heavy loam), sharp sand and brick or mortar rubble form the main ingredients.

As loam samples vary so much it is not possible to lay down any hard and fast recipe. The heavy loam would require more opening material such as brick or mortar rubble, sharp sand, etc, whereas the sandy loam would only need a small amount of these items. Soil lacking in natural humus would be greatly improved by an increased rate of peat and manure, so the following suggestion is intended for an average loam, and the reader should use his discretion and make variations accordingly.

Final Potting Soil

7 parts fibrous loam	1 part sharp sand
1 part decayed farmyard manure	1 part brick/mortar rubble
3 parts good horticultural peat	

The whole should be mixed well and to this should be added 110 g J.I. Base fertiliser and 20 g chalk lime per bushel.

Some years ago it was considered that peat was detrimental to carnation culture. It was said that peat made soil sour or lowered its pH, i.e. increased soil acidity. This view is no longer held.

The John Innes Institute concluded experiments on the most suitable soil mixture to suit most plants. They recommended:

> John Innes seed compost for seed sowings
> John Innes No. 1 potting compost for pricking out
> John Innes No. 2 for first potting
> John Innes No. 3 for final potting or bed compost

We used this formula for some years, making slight variations and additions, resulting in the above recommendations.

The John Innes Institute recommended a fairly high percentage of peat in their soil mixtures. Peat helps to open and aerate heavier or clay loams, and adds body and humus to sandy loams.

A small amount of charcoal added to any soil mixture for carnation culture is often an advantage. It is not quite known what role it plays in the soil, but it is believed to be a soil purifier and to absorb harmful gases. We make a regular practice of using it (approximately one 13 cm pot per bushel), and our plants do extremely well, producing a heavy crop of good quality blooms carried on strong stiff stems.

The more recently introduced 'soilless' composts have been proved excellent in the growing of carnations and other species of dianthus.

Next we get the potting bench ready, with the quantity of final pots required, a fair supply of clean crocks, i.e. pieces of broken pots for covering the drainage hole in the pot, and a rammer, which is easily made from a piece of broom handle some 23 to 25 cm long. Now we are all set for potting.

All plants, have, of course, had a thorough watering beforehand, and have had time to drain through. Place the pot before you and place a crock over the hole so as to form a bridge so that the surplus water may freely drain away. There is a right way and a wrong way of placing this crock in position. Often I have seen it put upside down so that it covered the hole but did not encourage drainage, for it almost closed the hole completely. Now partly fill the pot with the coarser parts of the soil, approximately half full, so that when we place the 9 cm soil ball in the pot the top of this ball comes level with the lower edge of the projecting rim. Before doing so, however, we use the rammer to firm the soil we have put into the pot, and when we put more new soil around the old ball this is also rammed, but care must be taken not to disturb the 9 cm ball as this would cause breakage of roots, and I prefer to leave the ball intact.

Should the plants have stood too long in the 9 cm pot and become a little potbound, then I would permit the base of the ball to be broken, but on no other occasion should this be done. However, if carnation plants have been attended to properly, and grown correctly, they should never become potbound, so there should never be any need for this treatment.

When the potting of the plant is completed, the surface of the soil should come to within 13 mm to 19 mm from the top of the pot and the old ball should be just visible (*see* Fig. 6). If we were to fill the pot with soil up to the top of the rim there would, of course, be no room for water, and it would be most difficult to moisten the soil if the ball became a little dry.

Obviously, after potting, all plants will have to be watered-in; all the soil should be thoroughly moistened.

We are nowadays tending to change over to plastic pots, which

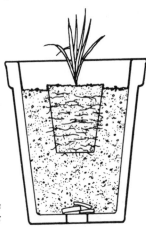

Fig. 6 A plant ex 7.5-cm pot, potted on into a 15-cm pot. Note the position of the old soil ball; also the placing of crocks to ensure drainage.

73

offer certain advantages over 'clays'. They are less likely to break, much lighter, easier to clean for re-use, and do not dry out as quickly as clay pots. This latter point has to be remembered if for years you have been used to clay pots, for overwatering could easily be the case. Whilst the soil surface in a plastic pot may give the appearance of being dry, the compost in the lower part of the pot could well be adequately moist and should not be watered. It is well to be careful with your watering until more experience is gained. Knocking the soil ball out of the pot from time to time, in order to examine the state of the compost, will help you judge how much you should water your plastic pots.

Planting Out in Beds

This can be done either from the 5 cm pots or the 9 cm size, but it is advisable to leave it until the plants are well established in the latter pot. They will by then have had the first 'stop' and should have formed a nice set of 'breaks' or side shoots.

As with potting, see that the plants receive a good watering well in advance. The soil in the beds should be slightly moist, as explained for potting soils, but it should only be slightly firmed, as I prefer to do all planting by hand and not use a trowel as we did when all beds were trodden down.

The next step is to mark the bed out, which is not absolutely necessary in the case of small areas, but the longer beds sometimes cause a bit of thought. There are many ways of doing this, and all I would say is: never overcrowd your beds, but give each plant sufficient room for its proper development.

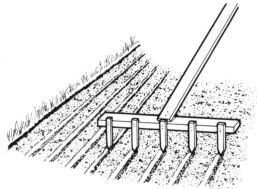

Fig.7 A home-made marking rake for quickly and accurately marking out rows when planting in beds.

The ideal spacing is 20-23 cm. The rows across the bed are spaced 23 cm apart, while the plants in the actual rows are at 20 cm distance from each other. On the other hand, planting 23 × 23 cm is quite acceptable, and with some cultivars which produce plenty of growth and foliage, this would be better. The bushier the plant the wider the spacing should be.

For marking out a bed quickly use a home made rake, with teeth 23 cm apart, to rake lines across the bed (see Fig. 7). Now, with a planting stick the width of the bed, with notches cut out at places where the plants are to go in each row, it will be a very simple matter to keep the rows perfectly straight.

Make a hole with the hand just deep enough to take a 9 cm soil ball which is placed in position with the surface of the ball level with the surface of the bed; soil is worked around this ball and the whole is pressed firm. A little loose soil may be left over the ball to cover it slightly and so avoid rapid drying out.

If the plants were watered well beforehand, watering-in will not be necessary immediately, except during bright, warm weather when a light damping down may be advisable.

Watering-in can be left for a couple of days; this may be determined by examining the ball which should not be too dry.

The soil ball should be examined occasionally and less notice taken of the surrounding soil. It may be necessary, a couple of days after planting, to water each soil ball in a similar manner to that of a small pot. A hosepipe with a short length of 6 mm pipe is ideal, as the direction of the water can be more easily controlled to keep the soil ball nicely moist.

This process needs to be repeated each time the ball shows signs of drying out. Depending on weather conditions, it may well be that this must be the method of watering for two or even three weeks, until the roots are beginning to get a hold in the new surrounding soil. Then it will be time for a general watering to moisten the entire soil contents of the bed.

Some two hours after watering it would be as well to test the soil in order to see if the water has penetrated deep enough.

The Use of Growbags

More recently, we have carried out extensive experiments to see if it was a worthwhile proposition to grow carnations in growbags.

We knew that tomatoes and other crops were grown very successfully in growbags, but those are only a one year crop, whilst we tend to grow carnations for a two year period. It was felt that growbag culture of carnations could offer a considerable saving on the high costs of steam sterilization of glasshouse bed soils, or the alternative complete resoiling of the beds.

As a result of our experiments, we now grow our perpetual flowering carnations, border carnations and pinks entirely in growbags, with outstanding results.

It is a method I can recommend to the amateur growing a fair number of plants. However, the growing technique is somewhat more precise as far as watering and feeding is concerned. A peat based compost such as that used in growbags is capable of retaining moisture, but once it has been allowed to dry out it is quite difficult to moisten again thoroughly. A careful watch must therefore be kept and water applied before the growbag becomes too dry. This is particularly important once an abundance of growth has been produced, which will take up more and more moisture from the growbag. During the peak of the season the growbags may well need to be watered twice a week, whereas during the winter once every 10 or 14 days is sufficient.

For growbag culture, I suggest that the growing area is first covered with black polythene, on top of which is spread a 5 cm layer of coarse peat. The growbags are placed upside down on the peat, and holes made in them at 4 or 5 regular spacings with a 4 prong garden fork. The growbags are then turned over into their permanent placings, so that the perforated bottoms are in contact with the layers of peat, from which they will take up moisture when required. The now upward facing top of the bag is provided with 4 or 5 slits across, the slits starting and finishing approximately 7 cm from the sides. We plant 3 plants into each slit, so each growbag will accommodate 12 or 15 plants, depending on how many slits we provide. I suggest only 4 slits for the more vigorous varieties, whereas for the 'Sims' I would consider 5 slits or 15 plants per bag.

It is not necessary to feed the plants in growbags until they have become well established. Then a liquid feed should be used, at the maker's recommended dilution, with every watering. A higher nitrogen feed is recommended for spring and summer, and a higher potash feed for the winter.

76

General Care

Watering

It is impossible to lay down any hard and fast rule on when and how to water. It depends on many things, such as soil used, weather conditions at the time, stage of plant, etc. It is more or less a matter of trying to understand the actual requirements of the plant, and in order to do this careful observation must be kept. This should not prove too difficult a matter for an interested grower.

After some experience, and by careful observations, the foliage of the plants will tell you a good deal as to the necessity of watering. Carnation foliage should feel crisp and brittle, but when the leaves feel 'leathery' it may be that they require a watering. First, however, the soil should be inspected, as it could also be due to other causes. For instance, in the spring, after the houses have been a little too warm during the preceding winter, the plants may become embarrassed on the first really sunny day and become limp, but an inspection of the soil may show that this is nicely moist. Thus, here again many points have to be considered.

However, the foregoing is a good guide. I could enlarge on this point by saying that a carnation leaf should snap when bent double between the fingers, but when it folds over like a piece of paper it is almost certain that the plants are dry at the roots, unless more serious trouble has affected the plant.

Testing plants in larger pots of moisture is best done by tapping the side of the pot with the knuckle of the finger, a walking stick, or a piece of cane with an empty cotton reel secured to the end, or any similar home-made device (*see* Fig. 8); a clear ringing note denotes dryness, whereas a dull noise which sounds solid means that there is sufficient water present in the soil and no watering should be done.

Plants in beds or permanent borders can be examined by pushing a clean, dry cane to a depth of 20 or 23 cm into the soil; if this comes out dirty, and with soil particles adhering, there is no immediate need for water, but should the cane, on removal,

77

Fig. 8 A simple but efficient instrument, made from an empty cotton reel attached to a cane, for testing pots for moisture.

be as clean as it was before it was pushed into the soil then it is time that watering took place.

We could also test the beds in various places with the aid of a long but narrow trowel, but care must be taken that as little damage as possible is done to the roots.

We experienced a good deal of trouble by the careless use of the trowel used for such a purpose, and have discontinued this practice. An ingenious idea was put to the test and proved very successful indeed. An odd length of 13 or 19 mm brass curtain rod, approximately 30 or 35 cm in length, was used to make the implement as shown in Fig. 9. By simply pushing it into the soil to a depth of 23 or 30 cm and giving a full turn, it can be pulled upwards, when in the cut-out portion the condition of the soil at varying depths can be quickly seen.

The natural growing period of the carnation plant is during spring and summer, and it is therefore natural that during this period more water is taken up by the plants. During spells of hot

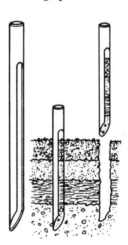

Fig. 9 An easily made soil auger. Left: the auger made from a 13 or 19 mm brass rod. Centre: the auger inserted into the soil to a depth of 23 or 25 cm. Right: the auger withdrawn, showing clearly the soil condition at varying depth.

78

and sunny weather the plants will transpire more moisture, which is taken up from the soil, and consequently the reserve moisture held by the soil will soon become exhausted if it is not replenished.

In our nurseries, for instance, it is sometimes necessary to water the beds in our houses, where carnations are grown for cut blooms, twice a week if the weather is bright and warm, while at other times of the year, when dull and showery weather predominates, they will go for 14 days or more without any watering at all.

I will say this, however; when we do water, we do it well, and this is a point all beginner carnation growers ought to remember. As an instance: on our nurseries, where our houses are 36 m long, we have five beds per house, all 1.2 m wide. The whole house takes approximately 4,000 plants, and on each occasion when such a house is watered we use 4,500 l. of water which is 1.1 l. per plant. I would not say that the quantity of water is measured out as exactly as this, but it is the approximate quantity for one good watering, sometimes it may be a little less, other times a little more.

Study your plants carefully and it will not be very long before you will understand the problem of when and how to water.

In the past, beds in commercial glasshouses were watered by using a 20 or 25 mm bore rubber hose, sometimes 18 m or more in length. Of course, as is now realised, this was by no means the best method of applying water to the soil. It used to be called 'flooding', and flooding it was. The soil texture on the surface was broken up, and after a heavy watering when the soil began to dry at the surface it formed a hard layer of fine silt, keeping air from entering the soil. Hand raking or scarifying was necessary in order to break up the surface so that air could penetrate the soil. How much damage was done to the roots, many of which were in the upper layer of the soil, is not known but I am convinced it was not the ideal way of watering.

It is much simpler today. There are establishments where the watering of houses can be done from a central point by merely flicking a switch. Hosepipes on a well-managed commercial nursery are no longer used.

On our own nursery, for instance, we can water each glasshouse of 30 or 36 m long by 9–10 m wide, i.e. 120–150 cm wide beds, by first turning on one valve and leaving this open for one hour in order to apply 4,500 l. of water per house, or 900 l. per bed. Some of the glasshouses are provided with time clocks and solenoid valves controlled by the clock. Such a system will, if set accordingly, apply water to the beds once every 24 hours so that, over a given number of days, the same amount of water is applied as would be given in one watering say, once a week, if operated by the chargehand by turning the hand-operated valve.

The system of water application varies from nursery to nursery. Each grower selects his own method to suit either his pocket or his nursery.

Lay-flat Tubing
There is first of all the lay-flat perforated plastic tubing. This is black polythene tubing, approximately 5 cm in diameter, usually available in rolls 150 m in length. The tubing is perforated by the manufacturer, or can be purchased unperforated so that the nurseryman can perforate with a special tool provided, at what-

A commercial greenhouse just after completion of planting. Lay-flat double-sided perforated tubing is in position, two rows per bed, for irrigation.

ever spacing he prefers. We like the perforations 75 mm apart so as to provide a more even water distribution and should, as sometimes happens, one perforation here or there not work properly there is little harm done.

Normally tubing is used with perforations at both sides, i.e. two minute holes each side of the lay-flat tubing. Two such tubes down the length of a 120 cm wide bed usually is sufficient, each tube being laid 30 cm from the side of the bed.

In practice, and especially in the summer when beds and the edges in particular dry out more rapidly, we prefer to use three tubes down the length of each bed, one double perforated tube down the centre, and a tube with one side only perforated along each side. This will usually provide more water along the sides of the bed to counteract the more rapid drying out along the sides.

The three tubes are connected to a metal or rigid plastic header tube at one end of the bed which in turn is connected to the mains supply. The other end of the tube is blocked off by just turning it over once or twice and securing it by means of a metal staple.

Trickle Irrigation
Another system is the trickle irrigation method. This consists of small bore rigid tubing, each with four to six or more specially designed nozzles at intervals to suit your needs, which are placed across the beds between the rows of plants. These laterals are connected to a 19 mm plastic or alkathene pipe laid along the edge of each bed which again is connected to the main supply.

This system differs from the first in the following respect. The lay-flat tubing provides a fine jet of water from the perforations which by valve control could be 15–30 cm away from the tube. The trickle irrigation nozzles emit water by a gentle slow drip.

Spray System
Another method which we have tried is 19 mm mains pipe along each side of the bed into which were inserted half circular nozzles which provide a semi-circular spray of water inwards only. The nozzles on each side of the bed were placed alternate to each other and approximately 1 m apart. Each reached the centre of the bed, but it is obvious that it left spaces of soil surface

untouched by water and plants in these spaces had to rely on water by capillary action.

We did not condemn this system because of this alone. In the main we objected, especially during late autumn and winter, to the excessive wetting of the lower foliage and because of this, this system is not in use on our nursery.

There are various other systems on the market all of which have merits on one score or another. Some growers design their own methods.

Ooze-tubes

There is another development, named the 'Ooze-tube', which is plastic piping stitched with a nylon thread along one side which, when connected to the 19 mm main along the side of the bed, will obviously leak or ooze from the stitchholes along the one side of the tube, the nylon thread preventing an actual jet. The principle of this system appeals to me, but our trials showed the application of an excessive amount of water. We are therefore experimenting with modifications.

We realise, too, that automatic watering for the amateur would be a boon, and there is no reason why it could not apply to use in an amateur glasshouse. We have seen one such system in use in an amateur carnation house for plants in 15 and 23 cm pots which proved to be practicable and efficient. It is called a 'Tricklemaster', and consists of a 7 m trickle line, with 20 adjustable nipples which apply 1.7 litres of water per hour. When each such nipple is placed to each pot, each plant will receive its share of water. A plastic heater tank connected to the water tap in the garden or greenhouse by means of a length of hose, fills at a slow, adjustable rate until a simple float valve releases the 1.7 litres of water. If required, the operation is repeated, or can be stopped after a single application.

Capillary Watering

Watering often brings from amateurs growing plants in pots the question 'Can I make use of a capillary bench to save a good deal of watering especially during the summer months when, often, watering may be necessary daily?' Such a system would undoubtedly save a good deal of time and is therefore widely used

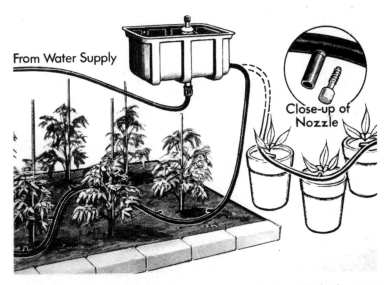

From Water Supply

Close-up of Nozzle

An ingenious yet simple method of bench or pot watering, making it possible for the amateur to apply the correct amount of water to his plants even during a period of prolonged absence such as a holiday. The rate of water to be applied can be accurately pre-set.

on commercial pot plant nurseries. The only difference would be that on such a nursery the pot plants are grown for a more or less short period, and as soon as they are ready are marketed, as is the case, for instance, with the flowering chrysanthemum pot plants. The carnation as grown by the amateur, however, would be in a 15 or 18 cm and later in an 20 or 23 cm pot for almost 18 months, and this is where the difference lies.

There is no reason why such methods could not be applied to carnations, although it must be admitted that the risk of spreading disease becomes greater, and it is for this reason that I am less inclined to adopt this method of watering for carnation plants.

The main principles for a capillary bench would be a perfectly level bench covered in one piece with heavy-gauge plastic film on which we have a layer of sand approximately 2.5 cm in depth. Water is delivered to the sand to maintain this at a constant moisture level, and plants in pots are stood on the sand so that the base of the pot is in perfect contact. For this culture the plastic pot with many slots and drainage apertures in the base lends itself extremely well, rather than the pot with only one centre drainage hole.

As already mentioned for crops which do not occupy the bench for too long a period, the method is ideal and saves a good deal of work, but for carnations I would not think it is the ideal way at all. I would much prefer a drip-feed system, but to date I do not know of a manufacturer who caters for, and makes, such a system for pots in particular. It would mean converting a Cameron drip-feed line yourself to suit the position of your pots.

Another system which could be converted is the Volmatic drip-irrigation line, which consists of a 19 mm short header fed from the main by a 1-mm bore plastic tube, from which are taken a number of 1-mm bore tubes of given length, one to each pot.

We have seen such a converted system applied to carnations in 15 or 23 cm pots very successfully and I suggest that anyone interested consult the manufacturers of the Volmatic watering system, as this method is fully patented, and I presume therefore that conversion can only be done with the approval of the manufacturer.

Winter watering
Watering during the winter months calls for the utmost care and attention. Needless to say the plants, owing to their inactivity as well as the natural moisture conditions prevailing, do not require much moisture at the roots. Evaporation is very much reduced due to lack of sunshine, and overwatering, coupled with artificial feeding, would produce unnatural growth which would be prone to disease. For these and other reasons, keep your plants very much drier, at the same time, of course, avoiding absolute dryness. The soil ball should always be sufficiently moist to maintain that healthy root system, and this motto should always be remembered: 'Water if really necessary and leave the plants alone if no water is required.'

A little at a time, as regular as clockwork, is, in all seasons, definitely wrong. When water is given to pots or beds, always give sufficient to penetrate the whole of the soil, but, of course,

84

your drainage must be perfect to allow the surplus water to drain away without hindrance.

Nutrients and Feeding

It has already been mentioned under previous headings that carnations, especially those grown in pots, require an occasional artificial feed. One should be careful with this, and wait until the soil balls in the final pots are well filled with roots, and the plants themselves begin to show their first flower buds. It is a mistake to think that a backward or sick-looking plant can be made to revive by a dressing of artificial fertiliser. The opposite may easily result.

Do not over-feed at any time. If a plant does not look vigorous and is not progressing too well, keep it on the dry side for a while, syringe the foliage occasionally with clear water, but do not feed on any account. It is only the healthy and vigorous plants which take the nutrients from the soil which must be replenished by artificial fertilisers from time to time.

Strong and robust plants are a drain on the natural nutrient elements in the soil, and if this is not made good by means of fertilisers, organic matter, etc, the soil will become exhausted. It is not always understood by amateur growers of plants that one can apply fertilisers to the soil without seeing any effect on the plants. This may be due to a sour soil in which nutrients would not become available to plants. I have already mentioned that plants not doing so well are best left alone for a while, especially as far as watering and feeding are concerned. Such plants will benefit by being kept on the dry side for a while to aerate the soil. By this I mean that a soil full of moisture cannot contain much air. Imagine for a moment the soil in the pot or beds as minute particles lying closely together, with very small spaces between each. These spaces are either occupied by water or air. If these small spaces are continuously being filled with water, no air is ever admitted to the soil to sweeten it, and the soil becomes sour. Air has the effect of conditioning the soil, and in a soil in this state, roots will form and the plants will thrive. Furthermore, in a very moist soil the plants will not form the roots which are produced more freely in a moderately dry soil, where roots will run out to find that moisture necessary to maintain the plant.

On many occasions, I receive letters for my personal attention from past customers who have at one time or other purchased plants from our nursery, and who write that the plants are not doing so well, although they admit that on arrival finer plants could not have been expected. They say that all the lower leaves are dying off, and they cannot think of anything to which this can be attributed. After making further enquiries regarding soil used, how and when the plants were watered, and so on, I learn that watering is done each morning before going away for the day on business. In my mind, there is then no doubt at all as to the cause of the trouble. Plants just cannot be watered according to the clock and with such regularity. It should be done only when required.

At our nurseries, we normally give the first 'feed' to our young plants some time in mid-summer. These plants were propagated during early to mid-winter, potted into 'finals' in early summer, and by mid-summer should have filled the pots with clean roots, and should be showing a number of flower buds. If in doubt, leave the feeding until late summer, when in nearly all cases the first dressing of an artificial fertiliser may be applied. Manure or soot water, diluted to the colour of weak tea, could be given as a liquid feed once every 14 days, and both will act as a stimulant from which the plants will benefit a good deal.

Chicken or pigeon manure, although very useful, should be used with the utmost care. Both are highly nitrogenous and would tend to produce soft and succulent growth and weaken the plant if not counteracted or balanced by another element. This would make feeding of perpetual-flowering carnations a very complicated business for a beginner, so it is best left alone.

Special preparations are easily obtainable from horticultural sundriesmen for feeding plants, but however good such fertilisers may be for lettuce, tomatoes or cabbage, I would not always recommend them for use on carnation plants. Each kind of plant has its own particular requirements, as have animals. For instance, you would not feed a horse or cow on pig swill, although the results obtained in fattening a pig with swill and barley meal are excellent; nor would you place some hay ready for a dog.

For lettuce, for instance, a nitrogenous manure which creates

86

The Cameron Dilutor, used for supplying nutrients via the irrigation system.

and encourages leaf formation would be ideal, whereas for beans which are grown for the pods they bear, a phosphatic fertiliser would be better. I do not say that either do not require anything else. All plants need nitrogen (N), phosphorus (P), potassium (K), and other elements, but some need more of one, and others require more of another. It has also been proved by scientific experiments that some plants prefer nitrogen in the form of dried blood, whereas others react better to sulphate of ammonia and similar materials.

It must be understood by now that carnation plants cannot be fed with anything bought in a bag from a garden shop. Always obtain a well-known brand of carnation fertiliser. There are several available, but use *strictly* according to makers' directions and do not increase the dosage recommended. Do not imagine, for instance, that you will cut twice as many blooms of double the normal size of flower if you increase the dose. It would be either a waste of fertiliser or, if you overdo it too much and too often, you will cause deterioration of roots and ultimately the collapse of the plant.

Remember that, during summer when watering has to be done

frequently, more so with plants in pots and to a lesser extent also with plants in beds, some leaching of plant nutrients is unavoidable and consequently the application of fertiliser must be increased.

It was not so very many years ago that a suitable carnation fertiliser contained a high percentage of potash. It was considered that a high potash feed was essential for the carnation plant. It was also common to believe that the feed used during the summer had to be different as far as the NPK rates were concerned. I do not believe this to be true today. It has been proved conclusively that carnations need nitrogen as much as potash, but probably phosphate to a lesser extent.

It is generally also accepted that a high nitrogen feed will tend to reduce split calyx, but this does not, of course, mean that a nitrogen feed such as dried blood or ammonium nitrate will cure your splitting problem.

I prefer a liquid feed to the dry feed, although there are reasons why from time to time we do apply a dry fertiliser as an occasional or supplementary topdressing to augment the regular liquid feeding. The reasons for this are as follows.

A liquid stock solution for application in a diluted form is made up of 'straight' chemicals which readily dissolve in water to supply the required nitrogen, phosphorus and potassium, the main elements for plant feeding. There are a number of minor or trace elements to make up a complete feed such as boron, magnesium and others, in small or minute quantities. The functions of some trace elements are still not fully understood. We know, however, that soild or powder fertilisers contain trace elements as impurities, and it is for this reason that I make a practice of applying such dry fertilisers to ensure that trace elements are provided from time to time.

Boron is one of the trace elements which, as far as carnations are concerned, is most commonly deficient, and for this reason borax is added to our liquid feed or nutrient stock solution at the rate of 250 g per 230 litres for ultimate dilution at 1 in 300.

Magnesium, too, is an essential ingredient, and this is added in the form of sulphate of magnesium (Epsom Salts) at the rate of 7 kg to a 230 litres stock solution mix, or 110 g of kieserite per m^2 of soil may be added when the beds are prepared.

88

Many growers prefer to apply adequate phosphates to their soil during the preparation of beds, or when mixing soil for final potting, and do not consider it necessary to add phosphates to a liquid feed. In such case a suitable liquid feed stock solution is made up as follows, giving equal concentration of nitrogen and potash plus trace elements:

17 kg of potassium nitrate
1.4 kg of ammonium nitrate
3.4 kg of sulphate of magnesium (Epsom Salts)
130 g of borax

dissolved in 115 l warm water; this would make an ideal concentrated sock solution, which can be applied at the rate of 1 in 300, providing 200 parts per million nitrogen and 200 ppm potash.

Although it is true that phosphates are the least likely to be easily leached from soil, I prefer to add phosphates to my liquid feed concentrate, and to the above ingredients I would add 3 kg mono-ammonium phosphate to have a complete nutrient concentrate.

There is little support for changing your feed from summer to winter feeding or according to season. The difference in water requirements between winter and summer will automatically result in less or more nutrient being applied.

As a matter of interest it is worth while mentioning here the nutrients removed by a carnation crop, of two years' duration, they amount to:

	kg per hectare per annum
Nitrogen (N)	130–160
Phosphorus (P_2O_5)	20–30
Potash (K_2O)	270–290
Magnesium (Mg)	45–65

From the above it may be seen and realised that supplementary feeding is necessary if we are to produce the best of which the carnation is capable.

Overfeeding, however, leads to dangers as well. It results in accumulation of salts in the soil (in technical terms referred to as

89

a low or high pC value) which causes damage to the finer hair roots, preventing the uptake of water and may, if severe, cause wilting of the plants. If this should be suspected it is best to water the plants really heavily so that the salts will be brought into solution and leached or washed out of the soil.

During the winter far less feeding is called for, and, depending on prevailing conditions, it could be discontinued. The temperature in the greenhouse should not be kept too high. During dull days, the boiler can be fired a little harder, but at the same time all possible ventilation should be given.

Extra boiler heat is required not so much to raise the actual temperature in the greenhouse, but to keep the air in the greenhouse drier by a better circulation.

It is possible that, during late winter, the plants are not quite as they ought to be, owing to the much shorter days and sunless winter weather, coupled perhaps with too high a temperature and overwatering. The foliage may not have that sturdy appearance of the healthy dark green foliage with that silvery bloom upon it, while the bloom stems cannot support themselves and hang limp over the supports. Such plants have obviously been forced and are best kept a little drier for a time. At the same time improve conditions generally, see that the glass of the greenhouse is clean and ventilate as freely as conditions permit.

If grown well during the winter, the plants should be well and strong and with the approach of better weather, more sunshine and light, they will soon show activity by the production of new growth. Then will be the time to give a spring feed. A light dressing of dried blood could be given, which should be followed a fortnight later by a dose of carnation fertiliser. From then onwards feeding the plants in their second year should be done, at first perhaps at intervals of three weeks, later more frequently. During the actual summer months a weekly application will be required.

Lime
Liming is occasionally necessary to sweeten the soil. Lime, although not actually a fertiliser, also assists in the liberation of nutritious elements which otherwise, although present in the

90

soil, would be of no use to the plants. Liming, however, can be overdone; some soils need more lime than others, but too much lime content will 'lock up' certain nutritional soil ingredients and withhold them from the plant.

After continual summer watering, the soil tends to become somewhat sour or stagnant, and during the autumn, therefore, it is wise to give the pots or plants in beds a light dressing of chalk lime. For carnations I always prefer chalk lime as this is milder in its action than, for instance, hydrated lime. A dressing of 60–120 g per m^2 would be the average.

Nutrient Disorders and Deficiencies
Nitrogen
The ideal soil level for nitrogen would be around 20 ppm. Soil levels around 10 ppm would produce nitrogen deficiency symptoms. Leaves and foliage in general would tend to become pale in colour. Another symptom would be the straightening of the leaves, i.e. the usual leaf curl would disappear and in general leaves would become narrower.

There would be a marked loss of 'breaks', and the space between the nodes would tend to become shorter. Stems become weaker, the flowers small, and in general the plant would look hard, with a pronounced loss of vigour. The greater the deficiency, the more pronounced the symptoms and in addition there would be a gradual loss of leaves from the base of the plant which will gradually creep upwards if the deficiency is not corrected. Calyx splitting would be greater than usual.

In connection with an excess of available nitrogen one would see a darkening of the foliage during the early stages of excess, and a tendency of the leaves to produce excessive curling and become rather fleshy. A soil level higher than 25 ppm would produce excess symptoms.

Soluble fertilisers, when applied carelessly, tend to build up salt concentrations, which discourage root formation and will cause damage to the hair-like feeding roots. If a build-up of high salt concentration is suspected, it is a good idea to water heavily on one or more occasions so as to render the salts soluble and leach them from the soil.

91

Phosphorus

The lower leaves of a phosphorus deficient carnation plant die off as the stored phosphate in the older leaves is gradually transferred to the younger leaves. As the plant continues to grow in a phosphate deficient medium, the phosphorus build-up in older leaves is called upon by the plant to sustain the new growth. Such a call will hasten the maturity of the old leaves, which will then stop functioning and gradually die off. This will continue until the deficiency is corrected, and could progress so that almost half the foliage from ground level upwards is dead.

It is therefore of benefit to the plants if such disorder is diagnosed correctly in the early stages and is corrected by an application of, say, triple-superphosphate at 110–140 g per m².

An overdose of phosphate does not seem to have very serious consequences except where the phosphate levels are very high, when such condition could contribute to calyx splitting and a falling-off of flower quality.

Potassium

Symptoms of potassium deficiency, among several others, include leaf-tip burn of the lower leaves on the plant. This leaf-tip burn can progress upwards on the plant, when often the leaf will also show off-white spotting, and a partial chlorosis becomes more and more evident. The smaller leaves on the plant will also show a more pronounced white spotting but seldom tip burn.

Calcium

When carnation plants are grown in a soil medium in which a pH level of between 6 and 7 is maintained, a calcium deficiency is most unlikely. In most areas, if mains water is used, the water will contain dissolved chalk and if an application of calcium carbonate (ground chalk lime) is used once a year I doubt very much if a deficiency would occur.

A deficiency, however, is most likely with soilless composts, or where large quantities of peat are used, such as a sand-peat compost, when the pH could well fall to below 5. The symptoms of calcium deficiency are leaf-tip burn but mostly, if not only, affecting the youngest leaves at the top of the shoots, quite unlike the leaf-tip burn we mentioned under phosphate and potash.

92

1 'Arevalo'

2 'Aspinal'

3 'Astor'

4 'Bailey's Spendour'

5 'Chanel'

6 'Clara'

7 'Clara's Lass'

8 'Cordoba'

9 'Crowley Sim'

10 'Dark Pierrot'

11 'Fragrant Anne'

12 'Jacqueline Ann'

13 'Lena'

14 'Miledy'

15 'Monte Video'

16 'Pierrot'

17 'Raggio di Sole'

18 'Red Runner'

19 'Roma'

20 'San Remo'

21 'Valencia'

22 'White Sim'

23 'Bookham Perfume'

24 'Christine Hough'   25 'Dainty Lady'

26 'Eva Humphries'   27 'Fiery Cross

28 'Happiness'

29 'Harmony'
30 'Lavender Clove'

31 'Lustre'   32 'Master Stuart'

33 'Merlin Clove'

34 'Anniversary'

35 'Betty Webber'

36 'Dad's Choice'

37 'Daily Mail'

38　'Doris'

39 'Granmere Pool'

40 'Haytor's White'

41 'Ian'

42 'Jenny Wyatt'

43 'Nan Bailey'

44 'Paul'

45 'Prudence'

46 'Sway Belle'

48 'Cartouche'

'Annelies'

49 'Ritmo'

50 'Rony'

Boron

Over-liming often causes boron deficiency, especially on light soils, and again in soilless compost cultures. A soil level of 5 ppm would be accepted as normal.

It is the youngest foliage which shows symptoms, as do the flower buds. The leaves become yellow and twisted, the terminal bud may die as a result of a deficiency, and the upper nodes would produce excessive ancillary side shoots. Often a bunch of negative growth is produced at some of the higher nodes; such an accumulation of bunched breaking is often referred to as 'witches' broom. Flower buds do not open normally but die off before they have produced any petals. Matured blooms become ragged and petals are abnormal. The tips of leaves of boron deficient plants show a dry, pale brown area with a band of reddish-purple, and with partial chlorosis of the leaf towards its base.

An application of borax (15 g per m^2) would soon correct the deficiency. My preference would be to use a liquid carnation nutrient which contains boron.

Boron deficiency causes the terminal bud to die and an excessive number of ancillary shoots to grow.

Magnesium

A deficiency of magnesium is not common on most soils which are or have been well manured. It is possible, however, on some soils, especially if potash is applied in excess, that a deficiency is created. The symptoms are chlorosis between the veins (yellowing) of the leaves, whilst the vein ribs remain green. An application of magnesium sulphate (Epsom Salts) should be given with a liquid feed, and here again I would suggest using a regular liquid carnation nutrient which contains magnesium.

First Stopping

By stopping, we mean the removal of the growing tip of the shoot, or shoots as in the case of the 'second stop'. I will first deal with the 'first stopping', given to plants either in the 5 cm or the 9 cm pots.

Some time after potting it will be seen that the plant has got 'hold' of the soil and is beginning to form new growth. Keep the temperature steady and certainly do not encourage—by high temperatures, artificial feeding or over-watering—too quick a growth of the plants. This would produce succulent and sappy growth, when it should be our aim to produce sturdy and vigorous plants, which can only be done by steady conditions, free ventilation, and a pleasant atmosphere.

Never 'stop' directly before or after potting; try and work this at least a fortnight before or after each removal. A young cutting potted into a 5 cm pot, with a single stem, will grow up and without stopping will run to flower quickly, producing one single bloom, usually of inferior quality and on a short stem. We have to promote a 'perpetual-flowering' plant and for this reason we remove the growing tip of this single stem plant, leaving from four to seven nodes, or sets of leaves, to induce the formation of 'breaks', normally one from each node. Thus a healthy, well-grown plant which, after stopping, has been left with seven nodes, should produce seven side shoots, forming an ideal and bushy carnation plant, producing, if left unstopped for the second time, at least seven blooms, on good stems and of good quality. A carnation plant can do even better than that, however, as will be explained when dealing with the second stopping.

At first it may be difficult, but I am sure that with a little

110

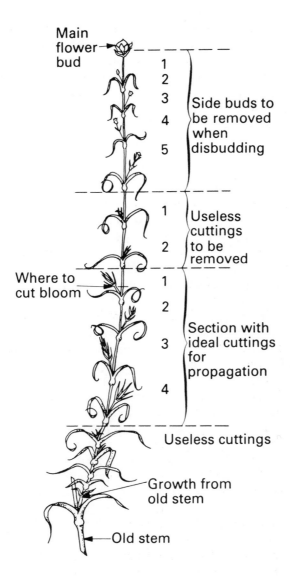

Main flower bud

1
2
3
4
5

Side buds to be removed when disbudding

1
2

Useless cuttings to be removed

Where to cut bloom

1
2
3
4

Section with ideal cuttings for propagation

Useless cuttings

Growth from old stem

Old stem

Fig. 10 A complete flower shoot from base to terminal bud.

111

practice, nothing will be easier than to break out nicely and cleanly the top of the shoot to be stopped. Hold the plant by the node, where it is intended to make the break, and with the other hand break the top of the plant sideways. Later it will be just as easy to do this operation with one hand only.

Plants propagated in early to mid-winter may, during mid- to late winter when still in the 5-cm pots, need stopping, but not immediately before they are to be potted-on into 9 cm pots. Usually when the young plant is some 23–25 cm tall, this first stopping is done.

Second Stopping

This is normally done when the plants are getting established in the final pots, or in the permanent borders. Some of the breaks resulting from the first stop will have grown away faster than others, and these we call 'leaders'. They are given the second stop first. Never at any time stop all shoots on a plant at the same time. Go over the plants once or twice each week and stop only one or two shoots, when ready.

Removing the tip of all shoots on any one plant would cause a severe and sudden check; besides, they would all form breaks at once, which ultimately would bring along a crop of blooms which flower all within a certain period, while later again we would have to wait for a further lot of breaks to supply the next batch of blooms. No, our aim should be to produce a constant supply of blooms and for this, as well as other reasons, we must do this second stop in stages as mentioned above.

Again, as with first stopping, we break clean at a node and aim at leaving from five to six joints, from which further breaks will come. When speaking of the first stopping, I suggested a plant with seven 'breaks' as a result of stopping. Supposing we stop only five of the leading shoots for the second stop, leaving two unstopped—usually the lower ones which do not grow as quickly—to run to flower. If each of the five shoots stopped for the second time produced four breaks, this would give us 20 breaks and two flower stems unstopped. So with early propagation, to give the plants an early start in the season, one could in this way produce some 22 blooms during the year. I must say, however, that this would not be the case with all cultivars.

No second stopping should be done from mid-summer onwards, and should the plants have become quite bushy after
stopping only two or three of the leaders it will not be necessary
to go on stopping up to that time.

Plants thus stopped will produce their first blooms some time
during late summer and continue flowering right through the
winter. If kept in good health and vigour they should produce
blooms for several years continuously, until the plants either
become too large to handle or die of 'old age'.

Commercial growers, however, do not grow their plants for
longer than two years, although some of them may keep them for
a three-year period; however, these have to be really good plants
and not too tall for normal and economic working.

There is a tendency nowadays for commercial cut flower nurseries to plant very much closer and grow the crop for only one
year—planting as close as 75 × 75 mm with only one stop. This
would not be a practice I would suggest to the amateur; even for

*Left: a plant in a 15-cm pot ready for the second stop. Propagated in late winter, by mid-
summer the leading shoots have elongated and are ready for stopping. Right: note how, in
stopping, the shoot is broken out and not cut or pulled.*

113

a commercial holding of average size, I would not at the moment consider it of real value, or a proposition which is to be recommended.

I consider that the amateur would get most out of his greenhouse by growing his plants for a two-year period. Longer than this would be fraught with difficulties as the plants would become too tall and the quality of the blooms would not be encouraging.

Supporting

We should now consider the best and easiest way to provide the necessary support for the plants grown in pots. The old way of doing this was to place a cane to each plant and tie every shoot with raffia at varying heights. Often the raffia would slip, come undone, or another tie was necessary at almost the same place. The result was an inadequate support for the plants, and an unsightly mess of bunches of raffia.

We now use a special support for all our pot plants; namely the two-legged supports for the initial stage before a cane really needs to be used. A 75 or 90 cm cane alongside each small plant some 15 or 18 cm high would look quite out of place and by means of our special support, made of special spring steel wire, the use of canes can be left until a much later date, while the use of raffia has been dispensed with for good. Any shoots growing outside this support's circle can at any time easily be tucked in, and the plants are kept quite tidy and neat. When it becomes necessary to have another support a little higher than the first, we make use of a thin cane, or better still a thin galvanised steel stake especially supplied for this purpose. The latter, of course, is much neater and does not in the least detract from the beauty of the young plants. Besides, they last indefinitely, unlike a cane which lasts no more than two or three years at the most.

Still, whether canes or steel rods are used, the method is the same. One is placed to each plant, which is by now in the final pot, and pushed into the soil so that it just misses the original 9 cm soil ball, i.e. some 5 cm away from the base of the plant. Onto this cane, or rod, is clipped a special cane-ring support which has a circle of approximately 15 or 18 cm in diameter, and embraces the entire plant. Another advantage of this support is that one can open its circle to bring within it any shoot which has found its way outside. It can be fixed at any height where it is serving the most advantageous support, and it can be raised or lowered at will. Thus one support is placed above the other as required and a neater and more effective arrangement could not be imagined.

For plants in beds or borders, the two-legged support is used in the same way as for pots. The next support, however, is different. At each corner of the bed an upright post is placed, firmly fixed into the ground and reaching some 1.4–1.5 m above the ground. Crossbars are fixed from the left-hand to the right-hand post at 13 cm intervals. The same is done at the other end of the bed, while all along the bed at 2.5–3 m distance a similar rack is placed, but of much lighter material, to carry the wires which are later run out between the plants the full length of the bed.

We use a galvanised wire of not too heavy a gauge for the centre wires, but the outside wires need to be a little more substantial as these have to be pulled as taut as possible. The wires are fastened at one end of the bed, the first layer of wires some 23 cm from bed level, and pulled at the other end where they are fastened to the corresponding crossbar. Now the wires are tied down to the intermediate racks and all is set for 'stringing'.

Use a fine cotton twine, and if the beds are the same width at any given point along its length it is a simple matter to cut a quantity of lengths off beforehand. Use a flat piece of board the length of just half the bed, plus approximately 5 cm, wind the string from the ball on to this piece of board and cut along the top so as to obtain a bundle of strings all the same length.

Fasten the string to one outside wire and stretch across the beds along each row of plants, twisting it round each thin wire as you work across the bed, and fasten on to the other outside wire. It would be very much easier if this work could be done by two persons, one on each side of the bed, and each one reaching half way.

In between each two rows of plants we have two strings, thus forming small squares with a plant in each one. It may seem an endless job, but really it is not so much trouble or nearly as complicated as it sounds.

As the plants grow, another wire exactly the same is placed approximately 13 cm above the first, and the stringing is done as before. So layer upon layer is added as the growth of the plant demands.

Disbudding

Perpetual-flowering carnation plants should be disbudded regularly. It should be our aim to produce one good bloom of firm substance and good shape per stem. To achieve this it is necessary to remove, when large enough to handle without causing damage to the main stem, main bud or leaves, all side buds and growth. All cultivars do not produce the same type of growth and differ widely in habit, so the following is a rough guide.

Disbudding should commence as soon as one can take out the unwanted side buds without causing damage. Often growers start disbudding too soon, being too eager to secure the largest possible blooms by doing so. To remove the buds and unsuitable side growth lower down the main stem is not too difficult, and very little harm can be done if these are removed by pulling them sideways and downwards. It is often with the smaller top buds that serious damage can be and is done. If they are too small to handle nicely, leave them until the next time you come round. Extra care must be taken especially with the bud directly under the main bud, for a slight mistake may damage the top set of leaves and so distort the position of the blooms, which will, through lack of support on one side, be inclined to grow sideways. One could even by mistake not only remove the unwanted side bud but also the main bud itself and lose a bloom.

One more point about disbudding, which is also worth making a note of for future flower cutting, is how far down the main stem one should remove all side buds and growth (*see* Fig. 10). This again differs with nearly every cultivar. Some produce long stems, others short stems, with cutting-like growth almost under the main bud and very few real side buds.

For cut blooms we must have stems sufficiently long, and therefore, with dwarf growing cultivars producing only short stems, disbudding should be done to your own discretion. Often one or even two side growths which would ultimately have

116

Disbudding. The stem of the bud is always broken away sideways and downwards from between the pair of leaves.

produced a good stem and bloom may have to be sacrificed in order to ensure a stem of sufficient length. This is especially the case with cultivars of dwarf and compact habit. The Sim varieties, however, produce a fairly long stem, even with the first flush of blooms, and disbudding has to be done to remove all definite side 'buds' and side growth below them if these are of an unsuitable type, being too thin and elongated, and having any appreciable length of stem between the lower set of leaves and the main stem.

If we look closely at an almost fully developed flower stem where the main bud is just about to show its colour, and no disbudding has taken place, it will be seen (as is shown in Fig. 10) that directly under the 'main bud is a tiny set of leaves from whose axil comes a tiny side bud, bedded closely in this joint. Lower down at the next joint, another side bud appears with a slightly longer piece of stalk attaching it to the main stem. The next one again has a much longer stalk attaching it to the main stem. The next one again has a much longer stalk and may even have a small set of leaves of its own, while below this there is either another side bud with two or more sets of leaves, or a side-

117

growth resembling a drawn-out cutting with several sets of leaves. This is the general rather than the strict rule. Each cultivar has its own particular habit of growth. All the buds or growths mentioned so far must be removed either to obtain the length of stem required, or in any case because they would not serve any useful purpose at all. Below the last mentioned growth it is possible to find a good cutting or successive flower shoot, but this can only be decided on the spot (*see* Fig. 10).

I should come back now to the uppermost side bud which we found bedded in the highest joints, directly under the main bud. This bud is partially covered by a small leaf, which does not seem of any importance, but in wrong or careless disbudding, and so damaging or removing it altogether, it is possible to distort the main bud, or cause it to grow one-sided. These two leaves support the main bud, and if this support fails on one side, it tends to grow that way and, at least from the show bench point of view, would be a worthless specimen.

Cutting Blooms

Carnations are best cut early in the morning rather than at the end of a sunny day. During the darkness of night the plants have recovered from the previous day's transpiration and 'exhaustion' especially if the day has been bright, sunny and warm. In the morning the foliage is turgid and brittle, and the flower stem will easily break at a node dispensing with the use of the knife. I prefer breaking to using a knife, even for cutting of flowers, so that we eliminate the possibility of transferring disease or virus from one plant to another which is a great possibility where the knifeblade is concerned.

If, however, a knife must be used, do not use it on 'doubtful' plants, and see that it is sharp.

Breaking the blooms is obviously done at a node, but when the blooms are cut it should be done immediately above and close to a node so that no appreciable length of stem 'stub' is left above it. Should this fact be overlooked, it will be seen in time that the large piece above the joint becomes infected with *Botrytis*, a fungus which will grow right through the next joint and, ultimately, may travel right through the stem.

The place at which to sever the bloom was more or less decided

118

when the flower stem was disbudded. It is at, or just above, the node from where the first good side growth springs, which is to provide the succession of blooms later on. Fig. 10 shows this.

It is interesting to keep a record of the production of each plant or cultivar, if many plants of one sort are grown. Commercial cut-flower growers do, and it gives them an exact idea of the economic value of each cultivar. It is often possible to discard the right cultivar as far as production is concerned, and yet increase the number of plants of a cultivar which is not nearly so productive. This should not worry an amateur grower, but records do create an interest and much can be learned from them.

The blooms are placed in deep cool water as soon as possible after they have been cut.

The lasting qualities of the blooms will depend on a number of factors, but not the least of them is related very closely to the way the plants have been grown. The more vigorous and properly nourished the plant, the better the lasting qualities of the blooms. The length of time blooms will last when cut depends on the 'starches and sugars' the cell tissues contain. It is on these 'starches and sugars, which by the absorption of water are converted into nutrients, that the life of the cut bloom depends. It is for this reason, too, that it is wise to freshen the water from time to time, but it is no use doing this without cutting 2.5–5 cm of flower stem off each time the water is renewed. The reason is that bacteria will cause the blocking of the water passages of the lower part of the stem, causing the water take-up to slow down, hence the slow-down of conversion of nutrients and the shortening of the life of the cut bloom.

There are of course various other reasons why perfectly good flowers do not last. There is for instance the stuffy and overwarm sitting room, which cools off during the night and subjects the blooms to abnormal temperature fluctuations. During the evening there is a dense smoke if all members of the family indulge in smoking. Large quantities of fruit, especially apples, adversely affect cut carnations, so avoid such conditions as much as possible so that you may have the best from your blooms and enjoy them as long as possible. Placing a penny in the water or an aspirin is of no real value. There are, however, flower preservatives available, and the best of these is Chrysal (*see* p. 154).

119

Pests and Diseases

The major insect pests which attack carnations are, fortunately, fewer than is experienced with many greenhouse crops. However, these few can cause tremendous damage and must therefore not be neglected. The most common enemies of the carnation are: greenfly (aphids), red spider mite and thrip. There are also earwigs, caterpillars, tortrix moths and others, but the latter do not cause so much trouble as the first three. Rust and leaf spot are the most common diseases.

Common Pests

With regard to pests, I have never yet met a carnation grower who has not been plagued with any of those mentioned above, but I hasten to say that with the present-day methods of control they should not cause the headaches they did some years ago.

Controls in the past, particularly of red spider, have been imperfect, with the result that damage was severe, and on commercial holdings was sometimes beyond repair. Burning naphthalene on trays suspended above specially designed lamps was the only way which seemed to give some measure of control, but the after-effects on the plants were sometimes equally disastrous. The plants hardened and this caused the loss of breaks.

Controls have gradually evolved, from syringing with water under high pressure which dislodged the insects and no doubt possibly drowned many of them, but a complete cure or riddance was never possible, to finally the use of powerful poisons discharged from aerosol bombs. Today, control is so much more effective and comparatively simple in its application that there is really no excuse for insects causing serious damage.

In all cases it must be realised that prevention is better than cure and treatment should be commenced at the first sign of the presence of any pest. A regular routine application in order to keep the plants free from any attack is better than to wait until the plants are infested.

120

Caterpillars

These do untold damage to almost any part of the plant, but mostly to buds and blooms. They vary in colour and habit a good deal, but all mostly feed at night. It is, therefore, some time after 10 pm that is the best time to find them at work. By the light of a bright torch it is easy to catch and destroy them. Sometimes, a few may be found during the hours of daylight but most of them will have withdrawn to the soil where they hide during the day. An occasional dusting with BHC 5% powder is all that is necessary; the BHC smoke bombs used for other insect pests will also keep caterpillars at bay.

There are, of course, many products by a number of manufacturers on the market which are available to the amateur grower at the many garden sundries shops and garden centres.

Pan-Britannica Industries Ltd (PBI) supply Liquid Derris which is effective against caterpillars, thrips, red spider, aphids and greenfly (*see also* the Appendix).

Tortrix caterpillar damage to a carnation bud. Note the damage right inside the bloom. The two flowers on the left are normal.

Earwigs

These are a constant nuisance and cause considerable damage to blooms. The oldest remedy known is to trap them in the same way our fathers used to do, namely, stuff flower pots with hay or dry moss, and hang upside down on canes at intervals among the plants. Each morning the hay or moss has to be examined, and, if earwigs have been troubling you, several are sure to be found sleeping, when it is easy to destroy them by steeping 'pot and all' in boiling water.

Although I have not heard any claims by horticultural chemists that BHC will kill earwigs, we have found at our nurseries that plants regularly dusted with this powder were not attacked by earwigs, while plants not so treated were badly infested with them. I think it well worthwhile to make a trial with some BHC 5% powder, should you get trouble with these little creatures.

A liquid Derris Spray has also been found effective, and another remedy which can be recommended as an alternative is 'Fenitrothion' by PBI, used as a spray in accordance with makers' instructions. ICI recommend the use of Sybol 2 Dust which contains Pirmiphos-Methyl. It is available as a puffer-pack, which is particularly useful when the usually very high humidity favours the use of dusts rather than sprays.

Greenfly (Aphids)

Aphids are small, soft-bodied insects which feed by puncturing the foliage and sucking out the cell contents, causing discoloration, wilting and distorted growth. If left unmolested they increase rapidly and excrete a sweetish, sticky liquid, or 'honeydew', which attracts ants, wasps, bees and flies, and which serves as a medium for the development of a black, sooty fungus. There are many species of aphids but those commonly found on carnations are the green peach aphids. Ladybirds, which feed on aphids, should not be destroyed, as they help in controlling the numbers of this pest.

Aphids live in colonies and are at first found on the underside of leaves and on the young terminal growth, when the adults give birth to living young; in the greenhouse this method of reproduction may continue throughout the year. Out of doors many species develop females which lay eggs. All the lice hatching from the eggs are females and are capable of producing young without the intervention of the male. The newly born aphids develop very rapidly and are very prolific. A single female may give birth to 100 young at the rate of from four to nine a day. Eggs may overwinter and hatch the following spring.

Fortunately aphids are easily killed. Formerly, some form of nicotine used as a spray or fumigant was a common control. It is still effective today, but plants should not be sprayed during spells of bright sunshine as otherwise the foliage will be 'scorched'. A temperature of 16°C (60°F) should be maintained for the best effect. Nicotine (96–98%) is diluted with water at the rate of 280 g of nicotine to 45 l of water, and if clean rainwater is available it is best to use this, as soft water will provide a better cover on the foliage.

I do not favour the use of soft soaps on carnations as this tends to spoil the 'bloom' on the foliage which, after frequent spraying with a soapy or oil solution, will be damaged. This 'bloom' is a waxy cover, or natural protection provided for the plant. A nicotine spray is best applied in the evening or during a dull day, but always ensure a greenhouse temperature of 16°C (60°F).

During prolonged periods of rain, when humidity is already high, and during the winter months I would not use a spray at all but rely solely on dusting the plants with an appropriate dust such as Lindane or apply a smoke bomb. The application of a wet spray would increase humidity still further and the plants would not dry very quickly. Damping off would be the result and conditions would be favourable for the development of fungus.

When using smoke bombs I need not stress the importance of a reasonably smoke-proof greenhouse. The size of the smoke bomb is calculated on the cubic capacity of the greenhouse by multiplying length by width by average height (*see* Fig. 11). Large cracks or gaps should be temporarily stopped up to avoid smoke losses during fumigation, and here again the temperature during the process should be not less than 16°C (60°F) and if possible it should be increased a little, to as much as 21°C (70°F).

Finally, a more recently introduced phosphorus insecticide is Metasystox containing oxydemeton-methyl. This is an insecticide with a truly revolutionary application. It is 'systemic', i.e. it is absorbed in the sap stream of the plant. It is much safer to use

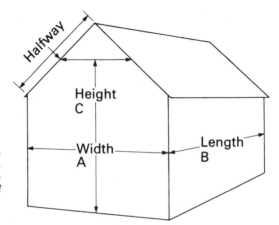

Fig. 11 The cubic capacity of a greenhouse can be calculated by measuring as indicated and multiplying A × B × C.

than other systemics and can be applied without the troublesome restrictions necessary with most phosphorus insecticides. Metasystox, however, comes under the Agriculture (Poisonous Substances) Regulations, and should be applied and handled with care.

It is an ideal material for soil watering. When watered on to the soil it is absorbed by the roots and carried to all parts of the plant. It is applied with the normal watering. When this material is used, the whole plant becomes poisonous to insects sucking the cell sap. Metasystox is mainly effective against aphids (greenfly) and red spider mites which are often difficult to reach by spraying, dusting or smokes, especially when foliage is damp. Plants watered with this material should remain clear of aphids for something like two months. It is claimed by the manufacturers that freedom from red spider could be even longer.

On carnations the rate of dilution is: 30 cc of Metasystox to 57 l of water. Young plants, i.e. in their first year, should be watered at the rate of approximately 9 l per m². Plants in their second year are watered at 14 per m². The best results are always obtained where plants are growing freely and growth is vigorous, because the uptake of the moisture is greater and more rapid.

As already mentioned, Metasystox is listed as a poison and care should, of course, be taken. It is advisable to use rubber gloves and a face shield when mixing the concentrate but protective clothing is not considered necessary when watering. Metasystox

124

should *never* be used on edible crops such as tomatoes, cucumbers, lettuce, cabbage and the like, whether under glass or in the open.

Metasystox is only available to the commercial grower, but fortunately, for the amateur grower of carnations there is a systemic insecticide available, and one to be recommended is made by the Murphy Chemical Co. Ltd (*see* Appendix for the address) named Murphy's Systemic Insecticide, containing dimethoate. It is applied in the same way as Metasystox and its efficiency is excellent.

We would recommend this systemic insecticide as the best available for amateur use for general insecticidal purposes, and especially for carnations, as it controls aphids, red spider mite and thrips, as well as caterpillars. Full directions are supplied with each bottle, and should be strictly adhered to; it is available from all garden sundries shops.

Red Spider

Red spiders are not spiders but mites, and are not always red, but may be greenish, yellow or brown in colour. They are minute insects about 1 mm in length. They puncture the tissues of the foliage and suck out the cell contents. These tiny punctures cause minute white scars on the foliage, and the sucking of the cell contents causes the leaves to become dull and to lose their blue-green waxy appearance and instead become dull grey. Eventually the leaves turn brown. The whole plant becomes weakened and stunted, and dies if nothing is done to free the plants from this menace.

In serious attacks, the mites first appear on the lower mature leaves, a careful examination under a magnifying glass showing them to be on the underside of the leaves. Masses of small white eggs in large clusters will also be noticed clearly. Before very long, and especially during spells of close warm weather, the entire plant is covered and the mites can be seen to move busily. They cover the entire bud and form a web over buds and leaves.

The experienced grower will know at once if his plants are infected by their appearance, long before he can actually see these minute pests.

The eggs, which under the magnifying glass resemble dew-drops, are deposited on the underside of the leaves and later all over them. In four to five days, minute larvae are hatched from them. These begin feeding at once and continue for about a day, after which they fasten themselves to the leaf and enter a resting stage for another day. The skin is shed and the primary nymph appears. This nymph feeds for a day and then enters a resting period of the same length. The secondary nymph then emerges and follows the same procedure. After the last resting period, the full-grown adult female emerges. She feeds for two or three days before laying eggs. At this time, mating and migrating takes place. Eggs are laid at the rate of six a day for the next eight or ten days. The female lives for about two weeks in a high temperature but may live a month at 16°C (60°F). Approximately six to eight days are required to complete development from egg to adult.

Adults are difficult to destroy and eggs even more so. After each spraying or fumigation, therefore, there will almost always be some adults and eggs left. The adults will soon produce more eggs and consequently, if an infestation is heavy, spraying or fumigating should be continued at five- to six-day intervals until there are no further signs. A 10- to 14-day application of a routine control measure will be about right if the plants appear to be free.

Materials used to control red spider are malathion (as for greenfly) and Sybol 2 as as dust or in liquid form for spraying. If sprays are to be avoided, a suitable alternative would be the use of smoke, such as the Fumite Smoke Cones (General Purpose Greenhouse Insecticide) by ICI.

There are still others on the market, but most of these are only available to the commercial grower because of their extremely poisonous nature.

Malathion as a spray or a Fumite smoke cone can nevertheless, be very effective. Care must be taken, however, in calculating the cubic capacity of the greenhouse in order to apply the correct dosage when smoke cones are used. It is also very important that the glasshouse is reasonably 'leak-proof', and that all cracks where smoke could readily escape are sealed up. It must also be mentioned that, in order to get the best possible distribution throughout the glasshouse, it is always better to use two or more smaller smoke cones rather than one large one, i.e. if the glass-house is of 18.5 m³ capacity, I would prefer to use smoke cones which together provide for 20 m³ or possibly even 21 m³. In such a case I would rather use three smoke cones of 7 m³ capacity than one of 21 m³.

When smoke cones have been used it may be observed that the 'kill' is not immediate and may take up to seven days. It is possible for the adult female to lay another batch of eggs before she dies and a further application some six or seven days later is essential. A temperature of 16°C (60°F) is necessary which should be maintained and, if possible, slightly increased for a period of three hours from the time the bombs are ignited.

It is during periods of thundery, hot and dry weather that red spiders manifest themselves all over the greenhouse in a very short space of time. It is, therefore, desirable to create conditions which are not favoured by these pests. Damping down the paths and greenhouse floors when the atmosphere is dry and warm is advisable so as to create some humidity in the greenhouse. Shading, and all possible ventilation to keep the temperature down, will also be of great help.

I do not favour, however, continual syringing of the plants themselves. This will give rise to outbreaks of rust and spot as well as encourage *Botrytis* and mildew.

Furthermore, keep your plants vigorous and healthy. It is invariably the poor, weak and undernourished plant which will be the first to be prone to infestation by red spider.

Finally, I suggest again Murphy's Systemic Insecticide as mentioned for greenfly. A systemic insecticide remains active for several weeks if watered on to the soil so that the plants absorb it through the roots, whence it will be conveyed to all parts of the plant, rendering them more or less proof against the attack by red spider as well as greenfly.

Soil Pests

Wireworms, leatherjackets, symphilids, eelworm as well as a host of minor soil insects can be destroyed by sterilising the soil with steam prior to planting or potting. Soil sterilisation by chemicals such as Novo (cresylic acid), Sterizal, etc, will also eradicate these soil-borne pests.

127

A typical leatherjacket, the larva of the cranefly. Leatherjackets can be distinguished from wireworms by the fact that they have no legs. They are also more greyish in colour.

None of these are found on the plants as are the previously mentioned insects, but are always in the soil. Wireworms in particular have a natural liking for lettuce, carrots or potatoes, but the damage they can do to carnations is very great indeed.

Wireworms bore into the base of the plant, causing the entire plant to collapse in time. It is often in new turf that large numbers may be found, where they are living on the fibre, but once carnations are planted or potted into infested soil, they are given preference, however much fibre there is present in the soil. Where the soil is used in beds, and time permits, it is always wise to bury at various places all along the bed pieces of carrot, just below the surface and marked with a little stick so that they may easily be found. On examining the carrot each morning, large numbers of these wireworms may then be caught and destroyed. I have also seen lettuce plants planted between young carnation plants, to act as traps for wireworms, but a piece of carrot is by far the best way.

BHC dust, raked into the soil four or five weeks before planting, is another means of clearing the soil of this menace, but the best and most effective method of dealing with them is steam-sterilisation.

Thrip

There are several species of thrip which attack carnations, but all are similar in habit and in the type of injury caused. They are minute, slender insects of not more than 1 mm in length. They move very rapidly and possess two pairs of featherlike wings. They are of many colours but at the adult stage are usually brown. Their mouth structure differs from those of red spider and aphids. First, they rasp the surface where they intend to feed and then suck the plant juices. This surface injury is more conspicuous than the puncture inflicted by spiders or aphids. If made on the flower petals, within the unopened flower bud, there will be white marks of irregular size on the flower petals when the bloom opens; if the leaves, or even the stems, are attacked, the rasped surface will heal and leave a brown scab.

Damage is nearly always done before we are aware of their presence and great damage is usually done to the blooms. Because thrips are so completely protected within the flower bud, it is very difficult to reach them with sprays or fumigants.

During the summer, and it seems to coincide with haymaking time, they fly or are blown into the glasshouse, so that even if a satisfactory kill is obtained another batch is likely to appear within a few days.

We make a practice (one that I would recommend to everyone who gets troubled with thrip) of dusting the lower parts of the plants and ensuring a reasonable cover of dust also over the greenhouse floor, bed or pot soil surfaces, with Gamma BHC Dust. In the south of England, we do this first in April each year as a precautionary measure and again in May. A final dusting is beneficial during the month of June. Thereafter a monthly spray until the end of August using malathion or Sybol 2 is a reasonable precaution. Murphy's Greenhouse Aerosol can be used as an alternative.

Nicotine spraying as recommended for greenfly can also be effective, but only against those insects with which actual contact can be made.

Thrips may lay eggs in the leaf tissue, or the females may pierce the buds and lay their eggs within the buds, where they hatch out in about eight days. During the period of development (from 10–20 days) these larvae enter a resting stage of from four to six days, after which the fully mature adult emerges.

While feeding, the thrip exudes minute drops of reddish fluid which later turns black.

Common Diseases
Mildew (Oidium dianthi)
A white powdery fungus, mildew is sometimes found during late summer, especially on buds and leaves, more often than not aggravated by dry root conditions; but directly the trouble has manifested itself it will spread rapidly under favourable conditions. Dusting with green sulphur and plenty of ventilation, however, should clear the trouble.

Karathane (dinocap) dust has been used successfully on our own crops. It is important, however, to dust as a fine fog, avoiding a heavy or uneven deposit on the plants. Apply at 10-day intervals, always using a perfectly still day.

Alternatively Karathane smoke bombs are obtainable, to make the application really simple. These should always be used at intervals of 10 days until the trouble has been eradicated.

Rust (Uromyces dianthi)
This has been known as long as carnations have been grown by man. Although it can ruin plants, it need not be a cause of fear for the grower, as so often is the case. It is caused by a fungus which thrives and spreads under certain conditions, and would disappear if those conditions were altered. Before applying remedies it is necessary to see that the conditions encouraging rust are removed; high humidity, continual overhead spraying and hosing, which causes the plants to remain covered with fine particles of moisture, are all favourable for promoting this disease. If, in hot weather, damping down has to be done as advised for red spider, do this before noon, or at any rate see that whenever it is done the plants will again be dry before nightfall.

Incorrect feeding or the use of an unbalanced fertiliser could also encourage rust, especially if such fertiliser tends to produce soft and tender growth as would be the case, for example, with nitrogenous fertilisers wrongly used.

Give plenty of ventilation, and keep the beds or pots moderately dry for a while, until improvement is noticeable. As a boy, I

130

Rust on carnation leaves. Raised, dark brown spots or blisters are produced, containing masses of spores which can rapidly spread to produce further infections.

can remember asking the foreman once: 'What is the cause of rust?' and his answer was: 'Bad growing, boy!' Many years of practical connections with carnation growing have proved his words to be absolutely correct.

Grow your plants correctly and no rust will trouble you. Here again, be observant, and learn to understand the conditions and environments in which a carnation plant thrives, and carnation growing will not be so difficult as at first imagined.

If troubled with rust, spray the plants with Bordeaux Mixture, or any colloidal copper spray, but, remember, this would be of no use if the conditions which encouraged this trouble in the first instance were not rectified.

A zineb spray or dust such as wettable or dry Murphane has been found very effective both against rust as well as spot. Use the wet form as a spray during summer and the dry powder form by means of a good dust blower during autumn and winter. Do it regularly, say, every 14 days during the latter part of the summer and early autumn, and if plants are clean, continue a monthly dusting throughout the winter as a precautionary measure.

131

A very good and effective alternative is Orthocide (captan), available as a dust or a spray. It is a very effective fungicide, but a preventative application is the best. More recently we have had the introduction of the fungicide Benlate, which is effective against several troublesome fungi attacks. It controls rust, spot, *Botrytis* etc, and is best used as a spray. Benlate can be used in combination with several often-used insecticides, and thus the two can be used in the same spray. The active ingredient of Benlate is 'Benomil'. Murphy's Liquid Copper Fungicide has also been used with success.

Leaf Spot (Alternaria dianthi)
This appears on the leaves in the form of a circular or slightly oblong spot—hence the name. It is easily distinguished; the centre of the spot is brownish in colour, with a darker ring, often purple, around it. Such spots can sometimes also be found on the stems, but this is not so frequent.

Plants left in the open too long after the summer can often be seen with this trouble. It is caused by similar conditions to rust, when the plants remain in a too-humid and damp atmosphere for a prolonged length of time.

It is wise to house the plants before the cold and damp nights give rise to conditions favourable for spot. Should there be spot on the plants, dust them with a fungicide powder, after all affected leaves have been cut off and burned. A dusting with lime and sulphur in equal parts is also a good remedy.

Another spot called fairy-ring spot (*Heterosporium echinulatum*) is not easily distinguished from the former. Light coloured or bleached spots appear on the leaves, stems, and on the calyx. On these spots, rings of black, spore-bearing bodies form. A second row of these spore-bearing bodies develops around the first and this may be repeated several times.

We have found that spraying with a zineb based fungicide such as Murphane, or dusting with a similar material, is most effective for both types of 'spot'. The alternative once again is Orthocide (captan) dust or spray. Here again I would recommend Benlate as a more recent alternative for the control of leaf spot.

Having said this, however, I must emphasise that both rust and leaf spot are caused by excessive humidity within the glasshouse, and it is obvious that to effect a lasting cure the cause of the trouble should first of all be corrected. This is best achieved by careful ventilation, ensuring adequate air movement around the plants. Sometime during autumn a little heat at the lower level will help to provide air movement. A small fan at floor level will have a similar effect.

Once it is known that attacks of fungi such as those mentioned are possible, it is always a wise precaution to dust at fortnightly intervals with Orthocide captan.

Stem-rots, including Wilts

One of the most dreaded diseases to have worried carnation growers for very many years is 'stem-rot'. When I first came into the serious business of carnation growing as a profession, there was not very much known about this disease. Every plant which died had either a decayed root system, or the base of the plant was diseased. In all cases the trouble was diagnosed as 'stem-rot'.

As the disease began to trouble carnation growers the world over, a great deal of research was undertaken in this country, in the United States and, in fact, wherever carnations were grown. It has been established that there are various types of disease hitherto termed as 'stem-rot'.

I feel that the following could be considered a 'disservice' to the prospective carnation grower, as it may create the impression that the culture is accompanied by so many hazards that it is almost condemned to death before it is undertaken. I hope, therefore, that a detailed outline will not be an ultimate discouragement as it is by no means so common an occurrence as it used to be, and besides, if your stock is obtained from a reliable firm where 'culturing' or bacteriological testing is a regular routine practice, the possibility of receiving plants likely to suffer from this kind of trouble is very remote indeed. Recent trials have shown that Murphy's Systemic Fungicide (Thiophanate-Methyl) has a beneficial effect on the control of wilts in carnations and its application (following makers' directions) is to be recommended.

The following diseases could be classified as 'stem-rot'.

Wet Stem-rot (Rhizoctonia solani)
Caused by a fungus which inhabits most soil and soil contami-

133

nated sand. It attacks a wide range of unrelated plants and is sometimes referred to as 'damping off' fungus. It attacks the plants at soil level, especially if the base is damaged by cultivation around the plants. The foliage becomes dull, losing its green colour. The entire plant wilts suddenly. Affected plants will pull away from the roots at soil level. The stem near the soil is wet and soft, the shredded bark sloughing off from the slightest twist, exposing harder tissues beneath. The roots themselves remain apparently in good condition. Brown knots of fungus mould may be seen about the decayed portion of the stem. The same fungus may also attack cuttings in the propagating bin or pan if the sand is contaminated and soil particles inadvertently find their way into the sand. Dirty seed pans or boxes in which other plants had previously been grown in soil would be a likely cause.

The disease could easily be confused with Fusarium Root Rot or Bacterial Wilt. Only a laboratory test could indicate with certainty which disease was responsible.

Spraying with any kind of material is useless, and effective soil treatment is not possible whilst the soil is occupied by growing plants. Affected plants should be carefully removed and burned immediately.

Bacterial Wilt (Pseudomonas caryophyllus)
This disease closely resembles Rhizoctonia and Fusarium Root Rot, but is not caused by a fungus. Bacteria enter the plant through the roots. The stem rots at soil level and the plants wilt rapidly. When the bark of the stem is removed, a yellow or brown discoloration may extend up into the branches. The inside of the stem at the soil line is yellow and slimy and feels sticky. The roots also feel sticky; this in both cases is caused by the bacteria.

Maintain the best and cleanest cultural conditions in and around the greenhouse. Again there is no spray which is of any use; no effective control has as yet been discovered.

Fusarium Wilt (Fusarium dianthi)
This disease usually begins with wilting of a single branch. The leaves become at first dull green, then yellow and finally straw-coloured. The affected branch dies and shrivels. Infection is at first localised in the stem or branch near the nodes. When such a

134

The carnation plants in the foreground are severely affected by 'wilt'. It is not easy to determine by visual means which of the wilts is responsible, as this can only be done with any accuracy by laboratory tests.

branch is cut lengthwise, the conducting tissue directly under the bark is found to be yellowish or reddish-brown, extending along the sap channel. Later, the brown colour will extend to the inner tissue of the stem as well as into the outer bark from the conductive tissue. When the stem is so affected, the branches on the infected side of the plant will wilt and die. Finally the whole plant dies. Infection is through roots or infected cuttings.

The inside tissue of the invaded stem is dry and of a dull brown colour, similar in appearance to dead timber.

Unfortunately, I cannot suggest any remedy or cure. The only thing which is certain is that the cleanest and most hygienic growing conditions will prevent trouble. In the USA, protective sprays have been introduced, but these are ineffective.

Obviously one should not propagate cuttings from plants which are likely to be infected or have been grown quite close to infected plants. Pot culture is most likely to confine these diseases to a single plant. Deep potting or planting should *always* be avoided.

Verticillium cinerescens

This is another of the wilt diseases; it enters through wounds, root tips and root hairs to attack plants of all ages, causing affected tissues to turn yellow and brown. Its presence is often obscured by the presence of other fungi, which also cause the stem to wilt and die.

If samples from such plants are taken for laboratory test, usually two or three wilts can be isolated, therefore it is not always possible to determine the primary infection.

The fungi are all more or less soil-born and wilt is more prevalent on soil where carnations have been grown for some years. The soil, therefore, must be sterilised by steam or chemical means, such as formaldehyde. Cuttings taken from healthy plants should be propagated in clean sand, and the additional precaution of dipping them in a colloidal sulphur solution would be worthwhile. Overwatering must be avoided as the fungi are favoured by overmoist conditions.

When handling plants for potting or planting care should be taken to avoid causing wounds or cracks to stem or branches, as such wounds provide entry for the fungus.

More could be written about wilts, but all of them are very similar and could not be easily identified without the means of a laboratory. Anyway, the ultimate result of each one is the same and for none of them, as yet, do we have a cure or antidote.

Physiological Disorders

Calyx Splitting

This is often looked upon as being caused by a fungus disease; I can at once ease your mind by assuring you that this is definitely not so; it is rather a physiological disorder. It could be due to many things. A review of carnation literature, and a study of reports from research workers and experimental stations, indicate that almost everything influences calyx splitting. It is now well known and recognised that the problem is due to a number of causes, several of which interact at times, and many fantastic explanations have been offered. I believe that the causes of splitting are: inherited characteristics; poor calyx formation; the increase in the number of petals, which may be influenced by temperature as well as other factors.

The formation of the calyx is a very important part and it is the responsibility of the raiser to take this into account when selecting the parentage for his new crossings. The calyx should be bell-shaped and have sufficient well-formed brackets to accommodate and support the petals as well as adequate 'spring' to allow for expansion.

An average cultivar will have 40–60 petals, although an occasional non-splitting cultivar will contain as many as 70 or even more petals. A cultivar with fewer than 50 petals and which still splits usually has a weak or poorly formed calyx.

Cool weather will cause an increase in the number of petals, not the following day of course, for the number of petals is established long before the flower opens. A cultivar which normally has 60 petals may increase to 70 or even 80 petals when subjected to low temperatures. This usually causes splitting. Consequently the autumn and spring are the two seasons when splitting is most severe.

Splitting does not occur until several weeks after the buds have been subjected to low temperatures. It is obvious, therefore, that after the summer, temperatures must be watched carefully, as during early autumn, when the winter buds are formed during times when temperatures fluctuate violently between day and night, this might well be the cause of splitting during the early winter. The same applies to spring.

It is also fairly certain that soil fertility and the application of fertilisers have a good deal to do with it. As mentioned elsewhere, it was always considered that the carnation required a good deal of potassium. Although this may still be true, it has been shown conclusively that the carnation also requires a high ratio of nitrogen. The cause of calyx splitting is aggravated by an incorrect ratio of potassium in relation to nitrogen. It has, in fact, been established by extensive experimental work that the carnation needs equal quantities of both potassium and nitrogen, and a suitable feed would contain around 180–200 ppm of both. If, therefore, a feed is used which provides, for instance, 200 ppm of potassium and 120 ppm of nitrogen, we would say that

On the right is a typical example of a split calyx. On the left is shown a thin metal ring, used to repair the split calyx. A metal ring, rather than a rubber band, allows the petals to develop satisfactorily.

this feed is out of balance, and it is such variation that causes calyx splitting.

Whereas you could use the correct and well-balanced feed, i.e. a feed providing 200 ppm nitrogen and 200 ppm of potassium, you could, without realising it, ultimately still produce an out-of-balance condition in the soil if the feed is a dry feed and it is used perhaps once a month, especially during summer. During that time of year watering is done fairly frequently, and if drainage is as it should be it must be realised that nitrogen, being easily made soluble, can readily be washed from the soil with the result that there would be an excess of potassium and a deficiency of nitrogen. It is because of this that I prefer a liquid feed to be applied in correct dilution with every application of water.

After a period of prolonged drought, a heavy watering may cause the calyx to split. Due to lack of moisture at the roots, the plant's tissues tend to harden and mature before their time, and with a sudden heavy watering further development of growth takes place, thus splitting the calyx. Also feeding with an incorrect fertiliser, especially when a heavy crop of blooms is just about to come into flower, could be another reason.

Any fluctuations of temperature, or conditions in general, can be the cause of excessive splitting of the calyx. There are cultivars which nearly always split their calyx at any time of the year, even if growing conditions are perfect; these cultivars ought never to have been introduced. No remedy is known, or could be recommended, and only good cultivation, at the same time avoiding fluctuating conditions, can minimise the risk of being bothered with splits.

Delay in providing heating in the autumn or discontinuing the heating in early spring in order to save in heating costs can be false economy. With a night temperature falling to 4 °C (40 °F) or lower, to −1 °C (30 °F), before we contemplate lighting the boiler and providing some form of temperature control, will lead to splitting and the formation of bull-head buds.

The same would apply where the temperature during the night was allowed to fall to a low level, and ventilation in the morning delayed. On a clear, sunny morning the temperature could rise rapidly to 21 °C (70 °F) or more after a night temperature of, say, 3 °C (18 °F), and this would inevitably produce splitting of the calyx, not immediately but after about three or four weeks.

American experimental work has shown that fan ventilation during the winter is a step in the right direction towards a better temperature control. However, the installation of only an extraction fan at one end and an air intake at the other is *not* the answer. The temperature within the glasshouse at the air intake end is considerably lower than at the opposite end. It was found that by the use of perforated polythene ducting some 23 or 25 cm in diameter, a better air distribution was obtained without creating a temperature difference, as was the case without ducting of this kind. Where such ducting was used the splitting of calyces due to bud chilling was almost completely eliminated.

Under miscellaneous causes one could include any combination of environmental conditions which cause a small calyx to be produced followed by large petals.

The calyx of a bloom is produced first. High temperatures at that particular time will cause the calyx to be small. Nitrogen deficiency, too, can cause a calyx to be small. If the cause of the

139

small calyx is corrected during the formation of the petals the calyx will split during the process.

Curly Tip

Curly tip is another physiological disorder which is not caused by a fungus disease. I must assure anyone confronted with this trouble that there is really no need for concern, and that there certainly is no question of disease. The plants will ultimately grow out of it with the approach of better weather and, in particular, better light.

Curly tip is more or less a seasonal occurrence. The first symptoms usually present themselves during periods of low light intensity and low temperatures (mid-winter to early spring). It is referred to by some growers as 'spring surge'. The plant wants to grow but poor light and other adverse conditions hamper progress.

The tips of young shoots fail to separate and continuation of growth results in a characteristic curvature. As soon as growing conditions improve, i.e. the lengthening of the days, more sunshine and better temperatures, the trouble will disappear. Artificial illumination has been tried but has not proved successful. Carnations do not seem to respond to such treatment as is the case with tomatoes or cucumbers.

On rare occasions we have also noticed this trouble at other times of the year and, in particular, on such cultivars as Sim types or those of similar habit, with long and fleshy leaves. It was found to be due to lack of nitrogen.

Undoubtedly, therefore, a nitrogen deficiency may also have a bearing on this disorder.

In winter the glass of the greenhouse should be kept clean, inside as well as outside. Keep the temperature fairly even around 4–7°C (40–45°F); a higher temperature would force growth and aggravate the trouble.

Should it occur at other times of the year, I would be inclined to suggest an application of a nitrogenous fertiliser, such as nitrate of chalk or dried blood, at the rate of $\frac{1}{4}$ teaspoon per 15 or 18 cm pot, after the plants have been watered, and the fertiliser slightly watered in. If curly tip is very serious and persistent during very early spring, a similar application could be tried on a

140

few test plants, but as soon as the trouble is corrected a feed with a general carnation fertiliser should be given.

Virus Diseases

The word 'virus' is derived from the Latin and means 'poison'. It has been used by the medical profession to designate infections and diseases for which there are no known causes. There are many theories as to the cause of virus diseases, but no theory has been proved to the satisfaction of all scientists. Because of this, many unknown diseases or symptoms in horticulture are called 'virus' as a quick and easy way out.

During recent years much more notice has been taken of viruses, their particular symptoms, their reaction on the plant, the effect on the blooms, and the effects on the cropping capabilities of the plants. A great deal more has yet to be done. It is known, however, that a badly affected plant will not crop as well, nor will the quality or the colour of the bloom be as good.

No evidence has been produced which would establish that viruses are carried in the soil, although they may be carried in the plants or in the roots that are left in the soil. However, they must be transmitted mechanically for they cannot move through the soil. The use of a knife when cutting flowers or making cuttings could, therefore, be one of the means of transmission. It is certain that greenfly transport the viruses from plant to plant.

The viruses are within the plant; therefore spraying would be of little use even if a spray was known to eliminate virus, but frequent spraying to control aphids (greenfly) will minimise the possibility of transmission.

There are a number of known viruses recognised today in connection with the culture of carnations. These are as follows.

Carnation Mottle

The vast majority of commercial cultivars show symptoms of this virus, the effects of which on the plant appear to be mild. Faint light and dark green mottling of the leaves is the only indication of the presence of this virus, although it may be that it also affects the rate of rooting of cuttings taken from plants badly infected. Once such young plants are established it will also be found that after stopping they will not 'break' as freely as those plants which come from a less infected stock.

141

It is not known with any degree of certainty how this particular virus spreads or is transmitted from plant to plant, and whether insects are mainly responsible, although it can safely be assumed that it can be transmitted by the worker's hands during the handling of plants. Carnation mottle virus is widespread and is found wherever carnations are grown. Research tests have shown that when literally thousands of plants were tested, all of which came from varying origin, every plant was affected to a greater or lesser degree.

Carnation Etched Ring
This virus is widespread, with symptoms similar to ring spot. These spots must not, however, be confused with alternaria leaf spots, which are somewhat similar. Young cuttings from infected stock often appear to grow out of it by producing clean growth or what may appear to be clean growth. Symptoms usually show more on older than younger leaves. It is also transmitted by aphids (greenfly). Normal handling does not appear to cause a spread of this virus.

Lucerne Mosaic
By no means common in carnations although it has been found in a few isolated batches. Transmitted by aphids (greenfly).

Carnation Latent
There are no symptoms of this virus in carnations but if found in combination with any other virus it will intensify the symptoms. Spread by greenfly.

Carnation Streak
Not often encountered in carnations in the UK. Streak symptoms, red or yellow in colour, are noticeable parallel to the veins, mainly on the more mature leaves. Details of possible transmission are not known.

Vein Mottle Virus
This is not frequently met with in the UK, although in the USA where it is known as mosaic virus it is quite common. As the greenfly is mainly responsible for its spread, we have found that

142

by careful and timely measures to control this pest vein mottle virus is kept under control.

Symptoms consist mainly, as the name would indicate, of a light green mottling of the veins. This is especially noticeable on the calyx. Dark green irregular streaks of the calyx are almost diagnostic for vein mottle. There is also conspicuous colour breaking of the blooms. This virus is very common on Sweet Williams in the garden.

Carnation Ring Spot
Most probably the most serious of the three common viruses (the other two being Carnation Etched Ring and Carnation Mottle) and, unfortunately, it is very easily transmitted during the handling of the plants. It may also be carried by the peach-potato aphid. Ring-like green or yellow markings on the foliage are produced, often with small dead spots, grey in colour. The leaves are shortened and distorted, with wavy margins, and these symptoms together indicate the presence of ring spot virus. It is found on a large number of cultivars, especially 'Joker' and the purple-coloured ones.

It is more than likely that other viruses will be discovered in the near future, as is always the case when vegetatively propagated plants are examined carefully; the surprising thing is that so little is known about virus diseases of so popular and widely grown a plant as the carnation.

On the credit side it must be said that cuttings from reliable sources, where strict attention is paid to hygiene and selection of plants intended for stock, should be substantially free from virus infection, with perhaps the exception of mottle virus, which can easily be missed where symptoms are mild.

Nuclear Stock Association
The earliest attempts to eradicate virus from carnation plants as practised by Dutch, Danish, American and British growers, were only partially successful. Some years ago a technique of eradicating virus from carnation stock was perfected by Dr M. Hollings of the Glasshouse Crops Research Institute. It was felt that the industry should derive benefits from this work, as trials

had established the advantages in cropping and quality beyond doubt. A meeting was arranged and all interested parties were invited to attend.

After all the preliminaries it was decided to form an Association, and with the encouragement of the Agricultural Research Council, the National Farmers' Union, and other interested parties, the Association came into being, and its title was the NSA (O) Ltd. A special unit, constructed at some cost, was erected on land leased to the Association by the GCRI, and has been equipped with adequate insect screening, fan ventilation, heating and sterilising equipment, and all necessary laboratory equipment. A close liaison is maintained with the GCRI on all scientific matters.

Stock of the very best clones of cultivars intended for cleaning are contributed by members, and all plants delivered to the unit are assumed to be infected, possibly with a fungal disease, and almost certainly with one or more viral diseases. Only unrooted cuttings are accepted, and only if an initial culture test shows them to be free of internal fungi. Such accepted cuttings are kept in a quarantine department, to provide material for meristem propagation, after which they are discarded.

Research work over several years, with stock produced at the Association's unit, has already shown that not only can one expect an increase in productivity of the crop, but the quality of the bloom, and very markedly its colour, is enhanced enormously.

Meristem Culture
The laboratory has been specifically designed and equipped for this work. 'Meristem tips' are obtained by dissecting buds (most of which will be dormant), down to the two youngest leaf primordia. A clean cut immediately below these removes the meristem tip which is then transferred to a test tube in which it is grown on, on a filter-paper 'bridge', dipping into a nutrient solution. The tubes are sealed without wafting in fungal or bacterial contaminants, and are stood under strip lighting, set to give them 18–22 hours' illumination in every period of 24 hours. Within a few weeks the tips should grow into viable plantlets.

Heat Therapy (Heat Treatment)

Heat treatment can free carnations from certain viruses, such as ring spot. Well-rooted young plants are grown on in high temperatures, 37–39°C (99–102°F) for a period of four to five weeks. After removal from the heat chamber very small cuttings are propagated from the shoot tips. Normally a large percentage of such cuttings are free from ring spot. The reason is that the plant grows so rapidly (produces new cells so quickly) that it outgrows the virus and the newest cells or growth have not had time to be infected.

Meristem culture, alone, or after heat treatment, can eliminate all the recognised viruses. The minute pieces of tissue cut under aseptic conditions and grown on in sterile cubes of nutrient consist of the meristem tip or dome, plus the first pair of leaf primordia. This tip or dome is no larger than 0.25–0.5 mm. The success of this technique appears to vary with the time of year and the best results seem to be during spring—the worst during autumn and winter.

Once the small meristem plant has grown into a sizeable plant under the strictest hygienic conditions, the utmost care is essential in order to avoid re-infection, and no efforts are spared to achieve this. During the growth of the young, virus-free plant, regular tests are carried out, so as to be absolutely certain that a plant completely free from known viruses is grown on, as future stock is to be multiplied from such plants by the registered stock producers.

The main methods of this testing consist of the following:

1) inoculation of suitable indicator plants which will show characteristic reaction if infected;
2) serological tests;
3) the use of an electron microscope.

The inoculation of test plants is very simple. It is also one of the most reliable means of virus detection. For test plants we normally use *Chenopodium amaranticolor*, which readily shows up mottle, ring spot, vein mottle, mosaic and other viruses.

A few young leaves from the carnation plant to be tested are ground up. The slurry so obtained is gently wiped on to the

145

leaves of the test plant and shortly afterwards rinsed off. If a virus was present in the carnation plant tissue the inoculated leaves of the test plant will show definite symptoms within from three to eight days.

Etched Ring virus is most easily detected by grafting to 'Joker', the cultivar which shows symptoms of this virus better than any other. It forms necrotic and chlorotic rings on leaves in three to five months. Streak virus can also be detected in this way in a similar period of time.

I should mention that the cleanliness, and the failure or the success, of any such scheme depends entirely on the painstaking care and thoroughness of the workers.

The NSA unit is responsible not only for the production and supply of virus-free materials to the registered propagators but also for the maintenance of this quality stock.

It will be concerned in supplying from time to time replacement stock, probably every two to three years, to the propagators in order to maintain the quality and reliability of the NSA stock cultivars.

We, as founder members of this Association, erected in 1969 a special insect-proof unit, completely isolated from the general nursery growing area, in which we grow stock plants obtained from the Association. These produce the cuttings for our nursery stock houses, from which we obtain our propagating material for our own plantings as well as for supplying our customers in the UK and overseas.

Preparing and Staging for Exhibition

This chapter will mainly concern the enthusiastic amateur carnation grower; the one who has been growing perpetual-flowering carnations for a few years, and considers himself to be fairly successful. This remark can often be heard at shows: 'My word, if that is a 3rd prize bloom, I have better stuff at home which would have given even the 1st prize a run for its money.' This is often true. It seems that it takes courage on the part of the amateur to fill in a show entry form, let alone to travel up to a show and stage blooms in competition. Why should this be so? The exhibitor surely does not stage his blooms with the sole intention of winning a prize! Surely the main reason for exhibiting in local or national classes is to participate in something in which one has a particular interest; seeing how your own efforts compare with those of others is secondary to this.

There are many advantages to be gained. You can see other cultivars, some of which may appeal to your taste for particular reasons. At the same time you meet people, all of whom have a similar interest, and all of whom are enthusiastic about your own hobby. Unless you take the plunge, you will not realise the fun, pleasure and advantage there is in being at a show for a day. I have attended shows for very many years, all over Britain as well as on the Continent, and everywhere I have made friends and acquaintances. Wherever I meet other exhibitors, we exchange ideas and experiences, and talk about new methods and developments.

Enter one or two local shows first and when you have gained some experience, venture to exhibit at some of the specialist shows, such as the shows at the Royal Horticultural Society's halls in London, where the British National Carnation Society hold their shows in spring, summer and autumn. In the UK, you will find also some excellent classes for carnations at shows like the Shrewsbury Floral Fête in August each year, the Southport Flower Show, and a number of others which cater specifically for amateur carnation classes.

147

If you begin by studying show results you will soon learn which cultivars are constant class winners. Take for instance the pure white 'Fragrant Ann', which almost always is amongst the first three; 'Bailey's Masterpiece', a deep velvet crimson, seldom meets opposition unless it is from another 'Bailey's Masterpiece', and so on. Once you know which cultivars you should grow for entering in classes, it is imperative that you obtain stock of these from the best and most reliable source. You can obtain cuttings from many sources, but the best of all would be from tested and cultured plants grown specially for the production of cuttings.

Having obtained the stock, provided the plants are grown in the manner described in this book, it would not be beyond the scope of any amateur to grow blooms of exhibition standard. It should then be your aim to stage them to the best advantage, and highlight the qualities for which the judges will be looking.

First of all obtain the schedule for the show in question. These are usually obtainable from the Society's Show Secretary. This will outline the classes in which you are permitted to exhibit your carnation blooms. There are in use specific terms, some of which perhaps need an explanation. There are for instance classes for 'novices' and 'amateurs', and 'open classes'.

The term 'novice' is usually described in the schedule. As a rule most societies interpret this as a person who has never won a prize before. Sometimes a novice is considered to be a person who has never won a 1st prize, so this would mean that anyone who has been awarded a 2nd or 3rd prize would still be entitled to exhibit in a Novice Class.

Again the definition of an 'amateur' is usually also stated in the schedule. It can vary from society to society. Sometimes it is stated that an amateur is someone who does not employ a gardener, and does not grow plants for sale or reward. It is important to read these definitions in order to avoid being disqualified.

Classes listed 'open to all' are just that. Anyone can enter, professional and amateur alike, as well as a novice who has the courage to do so, and feels that he has blooms which are as good as they could be. It is not unknown for a novice to clear the board, even when in competition with experienced amateur and even more experienced commercial or professional entries.

On further perusal of the show schedule you will see what to some may be a confusing assortment of classes. I cannot for obvious reasons explain here all possible show schedules. Let me take for example a schedule which gives classes for 3 blooms, and single bloom classes.

The first are classes 'open to all' and each class requires 3 blooms per vase. In this case, like most shows, vases are usually provided by the show society.

In my particular schedule there are 11 such classes, all of which are for 3 blooms, and 1 cultivar, as follows:

Class 1	White, 3 blooms, 1 cultivar	Classification A
2	Pale pink	B or C
3	Pink, cerise, rose	D
4	Deep salmon	E
5	Red or scarlet	F
6	Crimson	G
7	Yellow	H
8	Self apricot, yellow or buff ground	J
9	Purple, mauve, lavender or violet	K
10	White or pink ground	L or M
11	Fancy or self not fully represented to justify a special class	

Then we find on another page 1-bloom classes, marked 'open to members only'. You must therefore be a member in order to enter these classes.

Sometimes you will see 'open to any amateur'. This means that members or non-members can enter, provided they comply with the definition of the amateur grower as given in the rules appertaining to the society or show.

Here again the classes are similar to those above, except that only 1 bloom per vase is called for.

Another section of this schedule lists classes 'open to amateur' as follows:

Class 14	1 Vase, 3 blooms of not less than 2 cultivars
15	1 Vase, 6 blooms of 3 or more cultivars
16	1 Vase, 3 blooms of 1 cultivar
17	1 Vase, 6 blooms of 1 cultivar

Yet another section is devoted to 1-bloom classes, but these are open only to amateur growers, growing not more than 250 plants. The show organisers and officials rely on the exhibitors' integrity, and it is obvious that it would not be fair competition for anyone with 1 or 2,000 plants to compete.

The special 'novice' classes are defined as follows: 'Open to members who have not won a 1st prize at any of our shows.'

Class 20 3 Blooms any colour

21 1 Bloom any colour

The British National Carnation Society has compiled a colour classified register, so that it would be easier to list cultivars under specific colour headings for guidance of exhibitors and others. It was intended that each new cultivar upon registration with this Society, which represents the interest of the carnation in Great Britain, should be classified at that time and given the appropriate classification code.

The current perpetual-flowering carnation colour classification reads as follows: 'This list is simply a guide for exhibitors, intended to assist them in placing their exhibits in the proper classes. Only a few names of standard cultivars are given as examples. No examples are given for white, crimson and yellow, as it is not considered necessary to do so. It will be understood that under the influence of season, locality and culture, some cultivars of carnations change their colour in a more or less pronounced degree.'

Classification

A   All-white cultivars such as 'Northland', 'Fragrant Ann', 'White Sim'.

B   Pale pink cultivars, such as 'Crowley's Sim', 'Bailey's Splendour', 'Linda'.

C   Light salmon-pink cultivars, such as 'Monty's Pink', 'Paris', 'Laddie Sim', 'Lena'.

D   Pink cultivars, cerise or deep, such as 'Saugus Pink', 'Bailey's Delight', 'Viking'.

E   Deep salmon-pink cultivars, such as 'Shocking Pink Sim', 'Portrait Sim', 'Tetra'.

150

F   Red or scarlet cultivars, such as 'Majestic', 'William Sim'.

G   All crimson cultivars, such as 'Joker', 'Alec Sparkes'.

H   All-yellow self cultivars, such as 'Yellow Dusty', 'Golden Rain', 'Yellow Sim'.

J   Self-apricot or cultivars with orange, buff or yellow grounds, such as 'Tangerine Sim', 'Harvest Moon', 'Charles Allwood', 'Skyline', 'Dazzler'.

K   Purple, mauve or lavender cultivars, such as 'Deep Purple', 'Heather Pink', 'Margaret', 'Ruby Murray', 'La Royale', 'Blue Sydney'.

L   White-ground fancies, such as 'Helena Allwood', 'Arthur Sim', 'Red Diamond'.

M   Pink-ground fancies, such as 'Peppermint Sim', 'Brighton Rock'.

N   Cultivars, fancy or self, not sufficiently represented to justify a special class, such as 'Zuni', 'Dusty Sim', 'Monty's Pale Rose', 'Fragrant Rose', 'Raspberry Ice', 'Simstripe', all the Pelargonium types, any doubtful Pink cultivar not included above.

In most schedules for carnation classes there will be a specific instruction which reads: 'In any of the above classes, carnation foliage *only* may be used.' This rules out the usual plant foliage, including fern, other than non-flowering shoots of the carnation, showing out of or above the top of the case.

Other expressions are often included in the rules such as: 'All carnations exhibited in competition must have been grown by the exhibitor for at least three months [sometimes six months] previous to the show.' 'All cultivars must be correctly named. In case of close competition correct naming will be to the exhibitor's advantage.' 'Wiring of stems, non-removal of calyx supports will lead to disqualification.' I am sure that such simple rules as these will be easily understood, and will not be difficult to comply with.

We now come to the actual staging of the blooms for each entry. Experience gained and a knowledge of what judges look for will be a definite advantage and I give, therefore, to those who have never exhibited before, my personal views as to what I would be looking for as a judge.

1) The flower should be in a fresh condition. The petals should be turgid, without blemishes or travel marks. The colour should be clear, without fading, or discolorations due to cold or other cause.

2) The flower should be symmetrical and uniform. It should be of adequate size in keeping with the potential of that cultivar. Remember, it is not always and necessarily the largest bloom which will be considered worthy of the 1st prize.

   The form of the flower will receive critical consideration. Often one finds some petals more developed than others. This will diminish the shape and form, and lowers the quality of the bloom. I would not differentiate between flowers with serrated or smooth-edged petals, provided that the tips of the serration remain neat and regular, and have not been damaged in transit.

3) The guard petals, which are the outer petals of the bloom, should be firm and well formed. They should lie horizontally and preferably not curl down, as some cultivars will tend to do when the flower has reached optimum maturity.

4) Naturally the calyx must be round and unbroken. I would disqualify a split calyx, however good the bloom otherwise. I would also examine the calyx in close competition, and my preference would always go to a firm and well-filled calyx rather than a soft, badly shaped one.

5) The stem should be erect and strong. It is not necessary for the stem to be thick, but its strength should be apparent, and capable of holding the flowers in a perfect upright position. Then, in close competition, I would remove the flowers from the vase, and when holding the stem in a horizontal position by the base tip, I would expect the stem to remain rigidly horizontal. I would, of course, expect the foliage on the stem to be of good colour, free from blemish, virus infection or insect damage.

6) In classes for 2–3 or more flowers per vase, I would look for uniformity of all the blooms. Often in a class for 6 blooms in one vase, one would find 3 blooms of extremely high quality, free from any defects, with 2 blooms of a much lower quality and even 1 bloom of a very much lesser grade. Such an exhibitor would have been better advised to have entered a 3-bloom class with the 3 perfect blooms.

152

7) In a final analysis, I would consider fragrance. A carnation of good fragrance will always be admired, immaterial of its other qualities, and I would take scent into account, the more so when deciding between two otherwise very close entries.

The British National Carnation Society have laid down a system of pointing, with which one may agree or disagree. I myself would use the pointing system only as a last resort, or if I and my co-judge could not reach a final decision.

The BNCS pointing system is:

Condition	3
Form of flower	3
Substance	3
Fragrance	3
Colour	2
Uniformity	2
Calyx	2
Stem	2
Total	20 points

My own preference is as follows, in accordance with what I believe to be of major importance.

Condition	3
Form of flower	3
Stem	3
Calyx	3
Substance	3
Fragrance	3
Colour	2
Total	20 points

Uniformity would only be applicable in 2 or more blooms per vase, and I would allow a further 3 points for this, making a total of 23 points.

A further point worth taking into account is that it would be useless to have perfect specimens which by all standards should

153

reach top marks, if for sheer negligence or lack of knowledge such blooms were not staged to the best advantage. One should stage single blooms as well as vases for 3–6 or more flowers, so that the best is brought out and that the entry will immediately catch the judge's eye.

I think it was a great mistake when the BNCS decided to bring in the rule that the length of stem should not be more than 45 cm above the top of the vase. I feel that this should be left to the discretion of the judge, but while this rule remains in operation every exhibitor will have to comply. Yet it does not enhance the beauty of the flower as I consider that a perfect carnation bloom carried on a long, *strong* stem makes for real perfection. Look, for instance, at the Continental flower markets of Holland, Denmark, Germany and France, where commercially carnations are marketed with stems of 60 or 75 cm in length, perfectly straight and as stiff as 14-gauge wire.

However, when staging your bloom or blooms, always fill your vase fairly full with foliage, so that you can just get one or, in the case of 3 blooms per vase, 3 more flower stems in the vase. Do not forget water to the top of the vase, especially if you enter for a two- or three-day show.

If carnation foliage is in short supply I often use privet for filling the vase. This is cut with secateurs level with the top of the vase, and 3 or 4 pieces of carnation grass (non-flowering shoots) would be more than adequate to augment the flower.

The stem of the flower or flowers chosen for the class would be cut with a sharp knife diagonally so as to leave a pointed base which can easily be pushed into the filling of the vase; in doing so the blooms can be placed upright, showing off to good advantage the quality of the flower and rigidity of the stem, which will immediately attract the attention of the judges.

In order to have your blooms in prime condition for the show, cut the flowers one or maybe two days before the time they are required for staging. Preferably, cut them early in the morning and with a sufficiently long stem. The cut flowers are then placed in buckets or vases deep enough to ensure that at least half the stem is immersed in the water. I have found, too, that the addition of Chrysal, a Dutch product, which has proved to be a worthwhile flower preservative, prevents bacterial growth which fouls the water very quickly, and causes the stem tubes to clog, so preventing an adequate uptake of water.

This additive has proved to be valuable with carnations and a number of other flowers by prolonging the life of the cut flower. We have also found that blooms open better and develop better after standing in water to which Chrysal has been added. We make no secret of the fact that in staging our blooms for exhibits at leading shows we add Chrysal to water in all our containers. It is obtainable from florists and most garden sundry suppliers, but in case of difficulty I suggest contacting Trulls Hatch Products Ltd of Rotherfield, Sussex.

It is advisable to keep the flowers, once in water, in a fairly cool room and reasonably shaded from bright sunlight. In all probability your bathroom may provide the ideal environment where on warm and exceptionally dry summer days humidity can be provided by filling the bath with water so as to prevent a too-dry atmosphere.

Having mentioned this I should warn the exhibitor that once carnation blooms have been in water they are more prone to damage in transit. A flower which has been out of water damages less easily but, on the other hand, will not be in such ideal and perfect condition as the bloom which has been cut in advance and has had 24 or 36 hours in water.

So, great care is needed in taking the blooms to the show bench, as a damaged or marked bloom will be down-pointed considerably. Do not be tempted to hold flowers in water too long, either. Some colours will run or become broken quite easily after flowers have been in water some time, and this again will lead to the loss of many points.

Colours which are affected in particular are the heliotrope, burgundy or purple shades, such as 'La Royale', 'Mary Alesworth', and so on, as well as some of the crimson cultivars. Whites, too, could show a tendency to damp off in the flower petals if blooms are kept in water for some days and are then taken to a show for staging in classes.

I hope that the advice and recommendations in this chapter will be of some help, and in particular will persuade some to take the plunge to enter classes at shows. It is a great pity that more shows do not cater especially for carnations in their show schedule, but I am convinced that as soon as more of us embark on entering carnation flowers in show classes we will encourage show organisers to promote classes for our particular flower.

Hybridisation

It is well known that no two cultivars of a species are alike. The difference in habit, general characteristics, form of blooms, etc, are sometimes very obvious. Sometimes the differences are small, but nevertheless are quickly noticed by an observant grower. The hybridist utilises the variations between cultivars and species in his breeding programme, and predetermines plans in order to obtain better types.

Carnations, like other flowers, have both male and female parts collectively in one flower. The male part is the anther which bears the pollen, whereas the female part is the pistil, containing the ovary, style and stigma. Hybridisation calls for the application of viable pollen on to a receptive stigma.

When a stigma is in the condition suitable for pollination it can easily be observed. It becomes 'hairy' and begins to curl at the tip, at the same time it secretes a sticky substance which, however, may not be noticeable without a magnifying glass.

When pollen is brought on to such a stigma, either by wind, insects, or by hand, on a camel hair brush, or a piece of blotting paper, it adheres and may germinate, and from there will grow down the style to the ovary. The union in the ovary is called fertilisation. From the combined nucleus arises the embryonic plant.

The planning of breeding in the case of carnations is very complex, owing to a lack of knowledge of genetics of this particular flower, and even the well-experienced raisers can only be guided by past and long experience, and rely on judgment rather than knowledge.

Before attempting to 'cross' one should have observed and know intimately the characteristics of the two cultivars to be 'mated'. There should always be an aim or object. It could be an improvement of the stem of an otherwise excellent cultivar. By placing the pollen of the cultivar with the desired colour on to the stigma of the cultivar which excels itself in regard to its stem, the resultant seedlings *may* have characteristics which combine the two qualities, but I must add a word of caution. It is not as

157

easy to do as it is to describe, for otherwise new cultivars and very many new introductions would appear each season.

By interbreeding or 'back' crossing the best of these seedlings to either of the parents it could also be that the desired stem or colour is obtained from the second generation.

In my long experience I have found that there is no hard and fast rule either as to which parent one should use as the pollen bearer (male), or the seed bearer (female), as I have so often imagined myself to be at last on the track of something definite, only to find that by using the same technique the following season the complete opposite was the result.

The chances of producing an outstanding seedling are remote, but there is always that possibility of something exciting. I have had times when I have had three excellent seedlings out of one 'pod', but I cannot count the times that I did not have anything worthwhile even out of 1,000 seedlings.

Nevertheless, even for the enthusiastic amateur, there is a lot of pleasure to be had from 'pot-luck' crossing. The procedure has already been described above.

After selecting the parent male and female plants, the bloom to be used to bear the seed (female) must first be 'emasculated'. As soon as the flower is developed the anthers or pollen bearers must be removed—a pair of tweezers would be the best appliance for this purpose—leaving only the pistils. Depending on climatic and prevailing weather conditions, the stigmas will be receptive some two or three days after this operation. The pollen should then be taken from the bloom of the male selected and brought on to the pistils. A warm sunny day should be chosen.

I have already referred to the use of a camel hair brush or a piece of blotting paper.

It should be remembered, however, that each time a cross is made a new piece of blotting paper should be used, and in the case of a brush this should be cleaned after each operation: one cannot always be certain that there is no risk of pollen contamination by pollen from the previously used cultivar.

A method which overcomes this would be to use a pair of forceps to take out the pollen-laden anther which can then be lightly rubbed over the receptive stigma of the selected and prepared seed-bearing plant.

158

Pollen-
bearing
anthers

Stigmas

Ovary

Fig. 12 A carnation bloom with all petals removed, showing the reproductive organs. The ovary, upon successful fertilisation, becomes the seedpod. Pollination is best done in early summer, in which case the seedpod can be harvested towards the end of the summer.

A matter of a few days later it will be noticed that the bloom petals of the pollinated bloom will have collapsed and are wilting. This is a sign that the pollination has 'taken'. Some three weeks after fertilisation the ovary inside the calyx will have swollen up, and the flower petals will have withered completely. It is now time to remove these altogether and open up the calyx so that the seedpod will be fully exposed to the sunlight. Obviously, a label bearing the date of pollination, and the names of the parent cultivars, has been attached to the stalk of each pollinated bloom. Such details should also be noted in a book.

Directly the seedpod has turned brown it will be time to harvest. The seed should be very dark brown or black in colour. It is best to store these in an envelope bearing the label or similar identification marks.

Seeds may be sown three or four weeks after gathering or may be stored for some time for sowing at a later date. I always prefer to sow my seed some time during early winter so that my first seedling will be coming into bloom by the following summer.

American Spray Carnations

The American spray carnation is truly perpetual-flowering, i.e. it produces blooms throughout the year, and its habit of growth is identical. It also requires cultural conditions and attention identical to the conventional perpetual-flowering carnations in every detail. Yet these carnations have a characteristic which warrants further explanation, and it is because of this that they differ from the conventional perpetual-flowering carnation.

As I have already emphasised, the American spray carnation will produce blooms during winter as well as summer. It is therefore justifiable to incorporate this new strain in this section on perpetual-flowering carnations. Cultural attentions are as described in the previous chapters. Propagation, potting, feeding, watering, soil conditions, and methods and means of pest and fungi precautions are applicable as for perpetual-flowering carnations.

What then is so special or what is so different? It will be seen that although each individual bloom is somewhat smaller (seldom more than 6 cm diameter), and perhaps not so full, there is more than one bloom on each flowering stem. This is the only difference. It is because of this that they are so attractive and lend themselves so well for general decorative purposes and make-up work, such as a corsage, a floral bouquet, or for decor which requires lightness and grace. They were described by the raiser as 'charming', and one of the first raised cultivars was most aptly named 'Elegance'.

The very first cultivar which came from an American nursery in Connecticut was, however, 'Exquisite', from which 'Elegance' was a sport. The raiser was Mr W. Thompson, a well-known grower who has his nurseries in West Hartford, Connecticut. This strain very quickly became popular with the American public and is usually sold in bunches of four to six stems per bunch, often providing a total number of 20–30 blooms. It is not difficult to imagine what an attractive and fascinating vase this would make.

160

At first, and remember that my original notes on this type of carnation were written as far back as 1960, only two cultivars were available, the already mentioned 'Exquisite' and 'Elegance'. The former is deep purple-magenta, paling towards the petal edge to almost white, whereas the latter is a most attractive rich rosy-pink also paling to white at the edge of the petals. Both these cultivars are highly perfumed with a delicate old clove fragrance, which has so long been associated with the old clove-scented cultivars of earlier days.

Since then, we have already established a very interesting 'sport' on our own nurseries, and at the same time more cultivars of this strain have been obtained from American sources which will widen the colour range of these carnations, all of which retain this branching habit. We have now for instance, stocks of a bright scarlet, a self-pink, pure white and even an attractive self yellow, which, together with the original 'Exquisite' and 'Elegance', provide an attractive assortment.

So much for the detail of cultivars and colours. Although I have told you that there is no major difference in the way one grows the American spray cultivars, as compared with the conventional sorts, there are, however, two fundamental and important variations.

The first is that the plants are only stopped 'once'. When the plants have been potted from the rooted cutting stage into the first pots, they are stopped by taking out the growing tip exactly the same as advised on p. 94. A well-grown and vigorous young plant will produce 'breaks' at each node quite freely. No further stopping is required, as was recommended for other cultivars, because this strain will break freely without further stopping and well before the ultimate blooms are ready for cutting.

The next point which constitutes the second variation is 'disbudding'. The American spray cultivars are *not* disbudded. To do so would defeat the object of more than one bloom per stem.

Instead of concentrating on the main bud which, by removal of all side buds appearing on the main stem from the nodes below the terminal bud, produces one large bloom per stem, the terminal or main bud is removed in this instance, leaving all lateral side buds which will, by the time they form and open their blooms more or less simultaneously, also produce small side

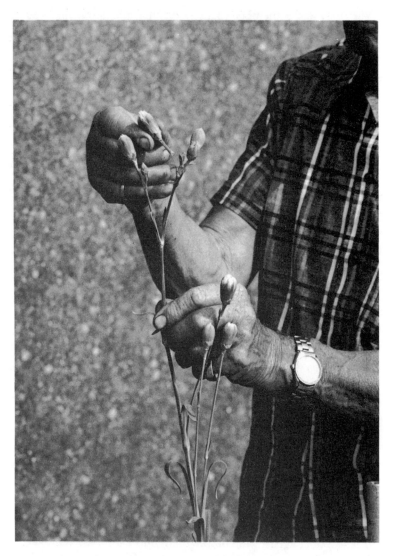

A typical complete flower stem of an American spray carnation, showing the elongation of the lateral stems, as well as the terminal bud, just showing colour. It is at this stage that the terminal bud is removed, as shown, to ensure that the lateral buds develop fully.

buds themselves, thus each stem making an attractive spray of from four to six open blooms as well as buds.

These cultivars are extremely suitable for pot cultivation, and the life of these cultivars as cut blooms is much longer than the perpetual-flowering carnation, no flower lasts better when used as a cut bloom for decorating the house.

I suggest that the water is changed once or twice during the week and approximately 2.5–3 cm is cut from the bottom of each flower stem, which is advisable in the case of nearly all flowers.

The half-open buds will open well while the stems are in water, and when the older blooms are removed after they fade, the newly-opened buds will maintain a fresh appearance and prolong the usefulness of the sprays.

Cultural Attentions throughout the Year

Winter

In the early winter, in the south we could now start propagating, and continue until early spring if necessary. Potting soils should by now have been mixed and be ready for use. Take care that such soils do not dry out too much; it is best to keep the heaps covered with a damp bag.

Occasional handling of plants in 15 cm pots is beneficial in more ways than one. By doing so, they will from time to time be turned, so that the part which was at first facing south is now turned towards the north. At the same time, the soil can be scarified, as well as limed, or dressed with a fertiliser as required. Dead leaves etc could be removed when handling the plants for one or other purpose.

Selection of cuttings is of the utmost importance. Remember that next year's results will depend on your efforts now, and that pains taken in the most careful selection of the best cuttings from the already-selected stock plant will be rewarded by the production of a clean and healthy succession of carnation plants. An inferior cutting cannot be expected to produce the best possible result, however good your further attentions may be. Even if cuttings, as may be the case on some cultivars, are not plentiful, it would be unwise to take whatever is going; it is better to wait a few weeks and then take some really good cuttings.

When ordering young plants or rooted cuttings to supplement your collection with something new, do so only from a well-known and reliable firm.

Remember, too, that for many reasons a good, selected stock of carnation plants cannot be expected to be cheap. The cost of maintaining a first-class stock is very great. Should you be led into purchasing plants, by lower price quotations, it will in the end prove to be more than expensive. Invariably, a 'cheap' article is, in the long run, dear; this is true with carnations more than anything else.

Mid-winter is the best time for propagating for those who have only a small number to do. Those with larger collections to maintain will have started earlier.

Plants in final pots should have some attention. Dead and old leaves should be removed, and the soil surface should be scarified. Watering of these plants must be done with the utmost care; avoid overwatering, especially at this time of the year.

Houses containing flowering plants should be ventilated as freely as outside weather conditions permit.

The days are beginning to lengthen and more light will stimulate more and better growth. We can usually also anticipate more frost, and attention should be paid to boiler or heating appliances so as to avoid low temperatures.

Compost for subsequent potting operations should be mixed in advance and kept under cover.

Seeds sown in early winter will need 'pricking off' into boxes or seed pans approximately 25–50 mm apart.

Towards the end of the winter, there will be an even greater increase in the hours of daylight and, although frosts may be heavy, gradually the sun will gain in power, and provide more suitable conditions in the greenhouse. Plants will show signs of new growth. Ventilation during the daytime should be increased according to prevailing conditions.

Cuttings propagated in mid-winter will be ready for removing from the sand after approximately four weeks from date of insertion, and should be potted-on into 5 cm pots, using J. I. No. 1 potting soil.

Flowering plants will benefit from a light dressing of chalk lime. Occasional spraying on suitable days will keep the plants free from insect troubles, especially greenfly, which at this time of year will soon make its appearance and become rather troublesome.

Cuttings propagated earlier will by now have rooted through nicely in their 5 cm pots, and to avoid them becoming potbound keep a careful eye on the amount of root developing in this small pot. Pot them on into 9 cm pots as soon as the 5 cm soil ball is becoming well filled with roots.

For later applications of sprays and smokes to combat any infestations of pests, make sure you have sufficient insecticides

165

by you to enable you to control them at the first signs.

If you intend to grow your plants in beds, commence the preparation of these in good time, in readiness for planting.

Spring

In early spring carnations to be grown in beds should be planted out into their final positions. Distance apart, and other planting details, are to be found under the appropriate headings.

Flowering plants in pots, as well as beds, should have a light dressing of dried blood, to be followed by a good carnation top-dress manure (see p. 71). Plants potted in mid- or late winter will now be ready for potting-on into 9 cm pots.

First stopping should be given to plants in need of this (*see* p. 94). As the weather improves, increase daily ventilation, and if possible leave a little air on at night, but at the same time do not overlook the possibilities of night frosts.

Watering should require more attention. The plants will need more during bright, sunny weather, less in cloudy, dull periods.

Continue your watch for insect infestation especially aphids (greenfly) and spray periodically as a preventative measure.

Potting-on should be done when plants in 5 cm pots are well rooted through. With improvement in the weather and general conditions normally expected at this time of the year, it will be found that plants require more water, especially those in large pots.

Earlier potted plants, now well rooted through in the 9 cm pots and forming nice breaks at every joint after the first stopping, can be potted-on into finals, i.e. 15 or 18 cm pots.

One-year-old flowering plants, those which were propagated the previous year and have been overwintered in the large pots, should now be potted-on into 23 cm pots. The same soil mixture as for final potting would be in order. Regular feeding of older plants is necessary.

Growth of plants will become more rapid now, and disbudding will be necessary more frequently. Go over the plants each week, and remove all unwanted side buds and growth.

Plants potted this season in final pots will soon require second stopping, but do not be too hasty with this. Wait until the shoots

166

to be stopped attain sufficient length, some 22–25 cm, and remove the growing tip (as directed on p. 94).

Further batches of plants now rooted through in 9 cm pots will again require potting-on into finals.

Towards the end of spring and beginning of summer, plants could be placed in cold frames which are covered with lights at night, but, during favourable weather, are opened up during daytime.

Keep up regular insecticidal spraying. During hot weather, damp down all paths in the greenhouse as well as under stagings, to avoid favourable conditions for red spider infestations.

No more fire-heat should be necessary, in fact, very often the boiler, or any other method used for heating the greenhouse during winter, has been discontinued for some weeks, depending on prevailing weather conditions. Boilers should be thoroughly cleaned out, removing all unburnt fire ashes; flues should also be cleaned, and the boiler itself should be washed out by means of a hose pipe. Dampers, flue doors etc should be left open while boilers are not in use. Door hinges, and all movable parts, such as flue damper regulators, should be oiled to prevent them rusting, and to avoid difficulty next season when perhaps the door may be found rusted up and difficult to open or close. All other metal parts of the boiler could be painted with a rust preventative paint.

Summer

In early summer, most plants will need some form of support, preferably two-legged. Our speciality is ideal as the first, but earlier potted plants now having had a second stop will need a second or even perhaps a third support, and a cane or rod has to be used, with a cane-ring support (see p. 114).

Plants in their second year should be fed regularly. An occasional watering with diluted manure, or soot water, is of great benefit. Plants potted into 'finals' this year, however, should not be fed with artificial fertilisers, but a watering with weak manure, or soot water, can be given from time to time.

This is when the first signs of red spider are usually noticed and a sharp look-out must be kept for them. Do not encourage this pest by conditions favourable to it; damp down all paths etc, avoid too dry an atmosphere, ventilate freely and, if necessary, shade the house with a thin coating of whiting on the exterior. This shading will prevent the undue fading of some cultivars which easily lose their colour during bright weather. If red spider has been seen, spray at once with malathion solution, or apply a Fumite smoke cone.

Further second-stopping of some plants may be necessary, but for autumn blooms do not stop later than early summer.

The summer show of the British National Carnation Society is usually held in July in the Royal Horticultural Society's Halls, London. Do not hesitate to send the Secretary your entry form, even if you have not shown before. If you can manage to go yourself to enter your classes for this first ever entry, ask the Secretary to put you in touch with someone with experience, as I am certain that there will always be somebody available eager to help you to stage your blooms to the best advantage.

Summer months may be the best for pollinating blooms intended for producing seed (*see* p. 158).

From mid-summer onwards, regular routine work will be necessary. Watering, feeding, supporting and disbudding of plants in flower, as required, will all need regular attention.

For blooms wanted during next winter, this is the last time for the second stop. No more stopping should take place after midsummer.

Free ventilation, with all possible side lights open, as well as doors, should be given; it may even be possible to maintain side ventilation, as well as top, during warm nights.

Do not forget the fact that carnations in their final pots can easily be grown outside, either standing on a thick bed of ashes, or partly sunk into the ground. The latter way will definitely help to prevent excessive drying out. During spells of hot weather, see that the shading is adequate—it may have been removed by a recent shower.

This month there will be a great influx of disbudding. Get it done on every possible occasion, especially if you are fortunate enough to be able to look forward to your annual holiday. Once disbudding and such jobs get behind, it will be difficult to catch up. Also in preparation for the holiday absence, arrange with some kind and understanding neighbour to do a little watering

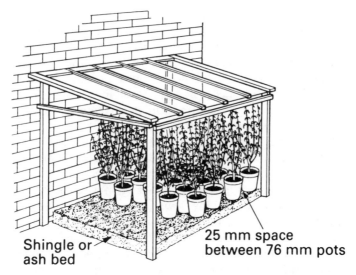

Shingle or ash bed

25 mm space between 76 mm pots

Fig. 13 A suitable protection which may be used for perpetual-flowering carnation plants during the summer months, so that the greenhouse can be used for a crop of tomatoes or other plants requiring greenhouse protection.

for you and to open the ventilators. Get him to come in once or twice beforehand when you see to the watering so that he will know better what is required of him. I am sure it will help him a lot, and you will be in a much better frame of mind when you are away.

As summer wears on, a light topdressing of a good carnation manure could now be applied to plants potted early in the year into finals. They will by now have rooted well through the soil in the pot, and should be showing their first flower stems, with, perhaps, one or two small buds.

Nothing more than the usual work is necessary. Support your plants adequately by adding, as required, another cane-ring support above the previous one; regular feeding of older plants should not be neglected.

Continue your look out for red spider and aphids, as well as thrip. Spray or smoke as suggested on p. 126, in particular for the red spider menace. This can be very severe if the weather is close and warm. Renew the shading if this should have been washed off and the weather is very bright and sunny.

Autumn

In early autumn, days will be getting shorter, and nights will gradually become cooler and damper; dew is often seen in the early morning. Should this be the case, it will be time to house all plants still outside. Do not do this in too much of a hurry, but prepare well in advance. Give the house in which the plants are to be placed a good clean-up; also clean the plants themselves, and prepare them for housing.

Plants potted this year into final pots should now be fed, and the earlier potted ones, fed for the first time last month, should have a second application sometime this month.

Last year's plants, now in 23 cm pots, must be kept clean, and if not specially required for flowering, could be stopped down in the early part of the month when, during the coming winter, they will produce an abundance of good cuttings.

When housing the plants, remember that perhaps you will be using some of them for propagation, and with this in mind it is as well to select the best, most vigorous and clean plants, to set aside for that purpose.

Should the weather still be warm, so that damping down of paths is still necessary, do so before noon now, in order that conditions inside the greenhouse are dry again by night.

We send out in 13 cm fibre terra-cotta pots plants propagated during early and mid-winter, and undoubtedly this is the best month to acquire such stock.

Lift fibrous maiden loam, and stack, grass downwards, with alternative layers of manure, together with a sprinkle of bone-meal and chalk lime, for use next potting season. Select the best possible soil, and see that there is plenty of fibre which, when rotted down well, will make ideal soil for carnation work.

Sterilise empty pots, boxes etc which will be required next season, with formaldehyde to allow plenty of time for this important operation. It will now be time to gather the seedpods from the summer pollinations.

Watering and ventilation will require greater care from now on. Heating apparatus needs to be looked over and it may be as well to try it out for a day to make certain everything is in good order. We may have to start a little artificial heat around now, to dry the atmosphere which often becomes very humid.

Towards mid-autumn it may be necessary to re-light the boiler, or apply other means of heating to the greenhouse. It will entirely depend on the locality, and if good weather is experienced, it is possible to do without fire heat for some time yet. In any case, it is as well to prepare, if not re-light. See that all pipes of the hot-water system are full of water and that there is no air-lock. If the system is supplied with a ball-valve cistern, see that the valve is working properly.

Maintain, as far as possible, a night temperature of 7°C (45°F) although we may have started to use artificial heat, continue with ventilation as freely as possible. During some periods of the day, even side ventilation may still be required.

It would now be better to use insecticidal and fungicidal dusts, or smokes, rather than wet sprays. Nicotine fumigating shreds are now preferred to nicotine sprays. Should sprays still be used, it will be found much more difficult to have the plants dry by night time, and rust may thereby be encouraged. Go sparingly with fertilisers. A dressing of wood ashes or ashes from the garden bonfire where hedge trimmings, etc, have been burned, is beneficial to the plants, owing to its slight potash content.

In late autumn, if the heating has been turned on, take care not to run an unduly high temperature; continue to ventilate as freely as conditions permit.

In the north, propagation could now start. Days now are usually dreary and winter is almost upon us. Growth tends to become more and more slow, and consequently watering must be done according to needs, and much more care and attention should now be paid to this. Do avoid high temperatures; 4–7°C (40–45°F) is quite sufficient.

Make sure all glass of the greenhouse is clean, and if necessary wash with a stiff brush to admit all possible light.

Thought should now be given to supplies of potting soils etc. This should already have been stacked, and have had at least one turning since stacking. It should now be brought under cover, because once wet it will take a long time to dry sufficiently to be of use for potting. During spare time, wash all pots to be used later on. Propagating pans etc should also be cleaned. A good, sharp sand for propagating purposes should be secured, and the propagating bin may require some minor overhaul.

Part II
Border Carnations and Pinks

Hardy Border Carnations

The true origin of the border carnation is not altogether very clear. Having researched in text books of years gone by, I still find the facts very confusing. The very earliest mention of the carnation I can find is by the Greek philosopher and naturalist, Theophrastus (*c.* 371–288 B.C.), known as the 'Father of Botany', who referred to a single five-petalled flower, pinkish in colour. The Greeks and Romans called it the 'Divine Flower' or 'Dianthus'. They used it in garlands and coronets for their champion athletes.

One reference suggests that the first carnations were brought to England around the time of the Norman Conquest (1066), either by deliberate importation by William the Conqueror and his knights from their gardens in Normandy, or by the seeds and roots being carried accidentally with the importation of Caen stone for use in building castles. In another reference book the author, Montague Allwood, mentions that, when visiting the old castles in France in 1937, he found an abundance of old *Dianthus* still growing in the remains of the walls of the old ramparts of Falaise Castle, the old French home of Duke William in Normandy. Evidence of these plants has also been found on the walls of old Norman castles in Dover, Deal, Rochester and Cardiff.

Clove pinks and thyme are mentioned in one book as being grown in the gardens of Henry de Lacy, Earl of Lincoln, at Holborn in 1286. In the year 1463 a painting of Edward VI showed the monarch holding a carnation flower in his hand. Clove pinks were also well known to monks as they were grown at their monastery gardens in all probability for making wine.

Chaucer mentioned the Dianthus in his *Canterbury Tales* of 1386 and gave them the name of 'clove gilofre'; this name was probably a corruption of the French *giroflee*, which most likely was derived from the Greek *caryophyllus*. The name used by Chaucer ultimately became 'gillyvors', and later in Shakespeare's *The Winter's Tale* 'gillyflowers'. The earliest date I have been able to find that the name 'carnations' was used was by Gerard in

175

his *Herball* (1597). During the Elizabethan period it appeared that the word 'gillyflower' was mainly used for the small feathery or plumed dianthus flowers, and the name carnations more for the larger flowers, although there never appeared a clear-cut distinction at that time.

It was during the seventeenth century that mention was made of specific cultivar names, namely 'Bristol Blue', and 'Granado'. Other cultivars were also referred to soon afterwards, such as 'Dainty Lady' (by Bradshaw) and 'Tawny' (by John Whittie). The colours ranged from white to bluish pink and red to purple... and blue. This latter is most interesting to me, for during the 50 or so years that I have been associated with growing, and in particular breeding new cultivars, I have never among my seedlings seen any suggestion of blue, nor have I ever heard that colour mentioned by other breeders in Great Britain or overseas. Could it therefore be true that at some time in those years gone by there really was a blue carnation?

John Parkinson listed thirty varieties of gillyflowers and nineteen of carnations in 1629. During the same period gillyflowers and carnations were mentioned throughout Europe, especially in Holland, Germany and France. In the early 1600s, many varieties were known to German growers; and during the reign of Elizabeth 1 the carnations and the rose were the Queen's favourite flowers, and were widely grown in the Royal Gardens. One well-known variety of that period was 'Painted Ladies', a flower with reddish-purple or pink markings.

During the reigns of James I (1603–25), and Charles I (1625–46), the most eminent and most often-mentioned carnation enthusiasts were Bradshaw, Fuggie and Whittie, referred to earlier. It was Henrietta of France, later the wife of Charles I, who gave fresh popularity to the flower by growing as many as 50 or more varieties in the gardens of Whitehall Palace. By the year of the Restoration (1660) 160 varieties of 'Painted Ladies' were listed, and by 1676 there is evidence of 370 varieties being catalogued. During that year too there is evidence of many varieties being imported from Holland.

By now the carnation had almost certainly become a florist flower. It should be remembered that up to this period the carnation was still mainly a garden flower, and it must have been the

Dutch who introduced the first 'bizarres', 'flakes' and 'picotees' into this country. These, as well as the 'Painted Ladies', remained as the florist flowers of that period up to the end of the nineteenth century. There are today few, if any, of these carnations in our gardens.

According to my research it seems that a Thomas Hogg of Paddington Green was the first man to write about the carnation in 1830. At that time there were several growers raising new cultivars in Britain and the carnation gained considerably in popularity. Another often-mentioned enthusiast was E.S. Dodwell, and it was he who really made the carnation a national flower (1877-80). There are records to show that meetings were held as well as shows, mostly in Mr Dodwell's private grounds in Oxford. These shows were mainly devoted to carnations. Rules were drawn up and the flowers are divided into sections. *Bizarres* had two colours placed longitudinally on white ground and were classed according to the most dominant colour. *Flakes* had one colour on a white ground and were classed pink, rose, purple or scarlet. *Picotees* had a white or yellow ground with the petal edges finely marked with another colour such as red, purple or pink.

Early in the nineteenth century Queen Adelaide, consort of William IV, grew a very fine collection of picotees at the Royal Windsor Gardens; hence the popularity of picotees at that time. Another author on border carnations was H.W. Wegnelin from Dawlish in Devon, who in 1898 wrote about foreign varieties and in particular about new French cultivars. Around the year 1900, Martin Smith was a well-known grower and raiser of border carnations. He was followed by Turner and Douglas who have left their mark, especially the latter, who became one of the best known breeders and raisers of border carnations of this century. Douglas of Bookham became a household name in the carnation world. He raised and introduced cultivars such as 'Bookham Joy', 'Bookham Grand', 'Bookham Belle', and others too numerous to mention.

A specialist carnation society was in being as early as 1916, known as The British Carnation and Picotee Society.

There are many who have done very good work in popularising and improving the carnation, not least an amateur by the

177

name of J.J. Keen, a resident in our local village of Sway, Hampshire, in southern England, where some of the older residents still remember the name. Fairley and Murrey are others who became well known. Of course there were the commercial names such as Allwoods of Haywards Heath in Sussex, and the firm of Douglas who by then were a commercial firm of note. We would like to think that we in Sway have done our share since 1940 in raising and introducing many new and worthwhile cultivars with improvements on the older types. I remember with a degree of satisfaction the very early cultivars I raised and introduced, such as 'Master Stuart', named after my youngest son, 'Leiden', named after the city of my birth in Holland, and 'Oma', named after my mother.

Soil

We are most fortunate to be dealing with a plant which could not be more tolerant as far as soil condition is concerned. It will accommodate itself in almost any type of soil, except waterlogged conditions in winter. We know, however, that in the lighter types of soil border carnations will give a better account of themselves, mainly because in the lighter soils the plants are normally assured of a good drainage. This is perhaps the most essential requirement in carnation culture.

If the soil is heavy and sticky, one can make considerable improvements to the texture by incorporating liberally a good horticultural peat as well as a fair dressing of a washed sharp sand, both of which will improve texture and drainage. Light sandy soils require plenty of organic matter, such as peat, well rotted farmyard manure or compost from the garden compost heap, in order to give body to the soil. A good strong loam which is reasonably open and free from stickiness with plenty of natural soil fibre would be ideal.

When preparing a border for carnations, or equally pinks, it is advisable to dig well and deep. Double digging in the autumn, leaving the soil rough so that winds and frost can act on it, is a sound means of obtaining a good texture. Digging over in the spring will be much easier. Add well-rotted compost or any other organic matter as already mentioned, as well as a dressing of bonemeal at the rate of 170–230 g per square metre. Better still, a dressing of John Innes Base Fertiliser at the rate of 110 g per square metre is all that is required. Just prior to planting, especially if it is suspected that the soil might be slightly acid, a dressing of chalk lime at the rate of 230 g per square metre raked into the top 8 or 10 cm would complete the preparation of the soil.

Choosing the site

I have already mentioned earlier that the carnation is a fairly tolerant plant, but if the best results are to be obtained the site for the carnation border should be chosen with care. It should not be overshadowed by tall hedges, shrubs or trees. Carnations do best in an open and sunny position; therefore choose a site where the plants will get the maximum amound of sunlight for the best part of the day.

As carnations, and as a matter of fact pinks, cannot cope with waterlogged conditions, especially in winter, I would always suggest making a raised border for these plants. A border with wooden, asbestos or brick sides would be ideal. For preference some 23 or 25 cm or more above the general surrounding garden level would ensure plenty of drainage and avoid any possible waterlogging during the wet winter season when so many plants are usually lost; not so much because of frost, because border carnations and pinks are reasonably hardy, but because of over-wet conditions around the roots, which is nearly always fatal.

Another cause of plant loss is the lifting of plants by frost. After severe frost the soil expands and lifts the plants. Afterwards such plants are left hanging more or less in mid-air and it is therefore advisable to go round the border after a spell of very frosty weather and firm the soil around the plants by treading.

When and How to Plant

The often debated question is when is the best time to plant border carnations and pinks in the open border. The answer depends on several things—mainly the climate and the type of soil. Although many cultivars are reasonably hardy once established, some do not stand up to severe frost all that well as young plants. Such cultivars are therefore best left for early spring planting.

179

In more southern regions with a relatively mild climate border carnations and pinks can safely be planted during October and even in the middle of November, which is better than spring planting, for under a normal season the soil temperature is still reasonable and the soil is not yet over-wet, especially in the case of raised beds or borders. Autumn-planted plants can then become established before severe weather conditions set in and will get away that much more quickly once growing conditions improve during early spring.

It is not always possible to have the soil in an ideal condition for planting during early spring. So often the soil temperature does not warm up to give young plants a quick start and all too often the soil is too wet for planting. In northern areas, where the winters are often much more severe, it may well be a case for leaving planting until spring, but in more favourable climates I would always get my planting done in late summer or autumn.

Now, for the actual planting, I will assume that the plants after propagation were grown on in small pots and are by now well rooted and ready for planting. As to pot size, this is less important; anything from a 5 to 8 cm diameter pot is ideal. If they are plants purchased from a reliable and reputed source, these too would be ex 6 or 8 cm pots. In both cases make certain that the soil ball is adequately moist, especially with the plants which have been bought in. These may have dried out during transit and should be stood in a shallow tray prior to planting to ensure that the whole of the soil ball is moist.

With the aid of a trowel, prepare the hole into which the plant is to be placed, but always make certain that the original soil ball is not planted too deep. Deep planting must avoided as this will lead to disease and the ultimate death of the plants. The surface of the original soil ball should be level with the surrounding soil when planting has been completed. As to distance apart, I would suggest that 23 cm between plants should be the minimum, whereas 30 cm would be needed for the stronger and more vigorous cultivars, especially if it is the intention to run the carnation border for several years. The soil around each soil ball should be fairly firm, and I would always 'tread' the soil of the carnation border prior to the commencement of planting so as to make certain that the soil is reasonably firm.

When planting is complete, all plants should be carefully watered-in, thus ensuring that the plants are well settled in.

Further Care

The average amateur is not always acquainted with what to expect. He should not be disappointed if during the first year of flowering each plant produces only one flowering stem, because that is the normal run of things. A small border carnation plant will, as soon as weather conditions improve, begin to elongate its centre shoot, which will continue to elongate, while at its base a number of basal shoots begin to form. There will be anything from 10 to 18 basal shoots depending on the cultivar concerned. Some are more prolific than others. The centre stem will ultimately produce a terminal bud with some buds below. More will be said about the side buds later under the heading 'Disbudding'.

The basal shoots during the first year are, if left alone, the flower shoots for the following year; therefore if the plant produces 14 or 15 basal shoots, apart from the flower stem, you can count on 14 or 15 blooms on that plant the following year, unless you wish to produce additional plants (in which case I would suggest that a number of basal shoots, preferably the strongest ones, are used for layering or propagation of cuttings in order to produce further plants to increase your collection).

Border carnations need little attention apart from staking and tying. In the first year a single cane would suffice for the single stem, when by using wire ties or sweet pea rings the stem can be secured to the cane. Frequent but shallow hoeing, more so during very dry spells, keeps moisture in and eradicates weeds. When the flower stem begins to elongate, in late spring, a top dressing of J.I. Base at say 55 g per square metre, or alternatively a similar dressing of fish manure, should be applied, and this should be lightly watered in.

During the second and subsequent years, in order to support a much bushier plant, a suitable support such as the 'cane-ring support' is required (*see* p. 114). During spells of very dry summer weather the border may need to be watered before the soil becomes too dry. Split calyx can often be attributed to a period of abnormal dryness followed by sudden and heavy rain. During dry periods do not be tempted to mulch border carnations with mulching material such as peat, straw or litter. This will encourage stem rot and harbour wood lice, earwigs and other damaging insects.

Picotee Borders

The cultivation of picotees is identical to that of the border carnations already dealt with. It has often been said that picotees are the less hardy types of border carnations; yet some would say that they are more hardy. They are easily distinguished from the conventional border carnation as they are always either white or yellow ground and are very delicately marked with a band of colour around the edge of each petal only. The planting, feeding and general treatment is the same as recommended for border carnations.

A few favourite cultivars to mention would be the following: 'Eva Humphries', most certainly the most beautiful of all picotees, white with a light purple band; 'Fair Maiden', white with a light scarlet edging; 'Firefly', yellow, heavily edged crimson/scarlet; 'Mrs J.J. Keen', an old cultivar, yellow-edged rose pink; 'Santa Claus', yellow with purple edging.

Flakes and Bizarres

A flake border carnation is a combination of two or more distinct colours. The bizarre border carnation however is always of more than 2 colours usually suffused one into the other. Here again these types are also treated and grown in the same way as all border carnations. Like all border carnations they should never be stopped, i.e. have the top of the shoot broken out, as is done with perpetual-flowering carnations and some pinks in order to induce the formation of side breaks. Both flakes and bizarres are far less plentiful today than they were during the early part of the century. The demand for them is now almost negligible.

Disbudding

Disbudding of border carnations will depend on what the plants are grown for. If you intend to exhibit, it is essential that you disbud, i.e. remove all side buds and side shoots below the terminal bud. However, do not remove all at once in one operation. Do it over a period, a few at a time, starting at the lower end of the flower stem, not of course the lower basal shoots which are the flowers for next year or which are used for producing new plants.

By removing side growth and buds a few at a time the risk of a split calyx will be greatly reduced. Leave the last two uppermost side buds till the very last, or certainly until one can determine what shape and quality the terminal bud is likely to be. Sometimes some faults or flaws can be detected when the terminal bud begins to open. It is then useful to have a replacement bud below so that we can remove the terminal bud and find that the secondary bud is as good or perhaps better than the terminal bud would have been.

If, however, the border carnations are grown for the sheer joy of a beautiful garden display, I would suggest that all side buds and growth from the nodes or joints of the flowering stem are retained, which will not detract from the quality of the main flower but will definitely prolong the flowering period. When the terminal flower begins to wilt and fade, it is removed, and the bud immediately below will begin to open and flower. When this one is past its best there is still another bud below this to carry on a worthwhile display.

Stopping

This is an expression well known by perpetual-flowering carnation growers, but it does not apply to border carnations. Borders need no inducement to form breaks. As mentioned earlier, the border carnation in its first year after propagation produces only one centre flowering stem during its first year. If we were to break out this single stem we would not get any flower during its first year and the breaking out of the top of the shoot would not result in the flowering of the basal shoots. So we would have to wait another year to see any flowers on such a plant.

Propagation

Border carnations can be propagated by either layering or by the propagation of cuttings. The older text books will only refer to layering of border carnations, and I have known many well-known border growers of years ago condemning the propagation of cuttings as far as borders were concerned. It was considered *the* thing to propagate cuttings of perpetual-flowering carnations as well as pinks, but never border carnations. Nevertheless, we have propagated border carnations from cuttings for many years with complete success, and the quality of stock leaves nothing to be desired.

The best time of the year for layering or propagation of border carnations would be soon after the earliest flowers are past their best, in mid-summer, although we often *propagate* cuttings in late summer.

Whether layering or using cuttings always select carefully the most vigorous and strongest basal shoots from the strongest and healthiest plants. Always remember that the quality of your young plants is only as good as the quality and vigour of the mother plants from whence they come.

The procedure of layering is as follows.

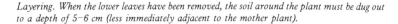

Layering. When the lower leaves have been removed, the soil around the plant must be dug out to a depth of 5–6 cm (less immediately adjacent to the mother plant).

The depression around the plant is filled with a layering mix (see p. 186), and when a layer has been 'made' it is inserted into the mixture (above). Approximately 3–4 weeks after layering, the connection between mother plant and layer is severed (below), so that the young plant becomes independent.

1) Select the strongest and most vigorous basal breaks.
2) Remove the lower leaves of each shoot to be layered except from that part of the layer which will be, once rooted, the young plant, approximately 8–10 cm in length.
3) Loosen the soil around the mother plant, shallow nearest the base but up to 5 cm in depth further away from the plant, and replace the soil thus removed with a layering mixture which is equal parts of finely sifted loam, sharp gritty sand or perlite, and a good horticultural peat, well mixed. No fertiliser or lime should be added at this stage. Make certain, however, that the new layering mixture is reasonably moist and is well firmed.
4) Have a sharp and pointed knife available and a supply of layering pins, which are easily made from pieces of wire approximately 10 cm long, which are bent over so as to resemble an old fashioned hair pin with the one side a little shorter than the other.
5) Insert the sharp point of the knife into the centre of the stem with the cutting edge facing downwards, one node below the lowest pair of leaves and draw the knife downwards, thus splitting the stem in half. Bring the knife out again two nodes lower down, making a 'tongue' which is trimmed immediately below a node.
6) This accomplished, bend the stem downwards without severance from the mother plant and insert the tongue and lower portion of the layer into the layering mixture and securing same firmly with the layering pin, bridged across the base of the layer. Make certain that the layer is in an upright position, still attached to the mother plant, and the mixture is firmed around its base.
7) When all the required layers are in position, water-in through a fine rose and ensure that the mixture does not dry out at any time. The frequency of subsequent watering will depend very much on weather conditions prevailing.

It will take from four to five weeks to root the layers, and in order to assist the layer it is advisable to sever the connection between mother plant and freshly-rooted layer say at the end of the fourth week. A week later the layer may be lifted carefully and will be ready for potting.

186

Planting Out

Assuming that layering was done in mid-summer, the rooted layer would be well and truly rooted by the end of the summer. If the new border intended for the new young plants was prepared well in advance, there is no reason why the rooted layers could not be planted in the position where they are to over-winter and flower the following year. The soil would be in perfect condition; the weather also would be ideal to establish the young plant quickly; so that by the approach of winter the plant would be well established and would over-winter well, provided that care has been taken in seeing that the site is well drained and not likely to become waterlogged during a heavy rainy season. Always plant carnations very shallow.

Potting-on

The best potting compost for potting young rooted layers, if it is preferred to pot the young plants for over-wintering in a cold glasshouse or cold frame for planting out in spring, is undoubtedly a John Innes No. 2. Use a 6 or 8 cm pot and always make sure that no more of the base of the layer is deeper into the compost than it was before being lifted. Always pot or plant carnations as shallow as possible, but see that the soil surrounding the base is well firmed. Once potted, place them in a cold house or cold frame at ground level preferably on a deep ash or shingle covered area to ensure drainage, and water the plants thoroughly. Then shade them by placing newspaper over them for the first four or five days during bright sunny spells, but dispense with shading at the first opportunity.

As soon as they are beginning to root and become established in the pot, provide all possible ventilation and light and grow them during the winter season fairly dry and hardy.

Propagation by Cuttings

This is a technique which fifteen or twenty years ago would be condemned, as it was indeed by several border carnation growers, when we started producing young plants, propagated by means of cuttings as opposed to layering. The 'experts' of those days maintained that only by layering could one produce strong and healthy young border carnation plants. However, from long experience, I can say without contradiction that border carnations can be produced by propagation of cuttings just as well as pinks or perpetual-flowering carnations can be produced.

It goes without saying that the cuttings to be propagated must be carefully selected and taken only from the strongest and most vigorous plants. As far as procedure, equipment and temperatures are concerned one can safely follow the propagating techniques suggested for perpetual-flowering carnations (*see* pp. 32–60) with the exception that they are best rooted in the summer, whereas perpetual-flowering carnations are normally propagated in winter and early spring.

Growing Border Carnations to Flower in Pots

Those growing border carnations for exhibition purposes would of course grow their plants in pots, for the simple reason that such plants can be given more individual attention, and if grown in a cold glasshouse can be protected from the weather. The plants, in 15 cm pots, are best grown completely cold. In the cold glasshouse they should be given all possible ventilation and during the winter watering should be at a minimum.

During spring, plants in 15 cm pots may be placed out of doors. In order to prevent worms from getting into the flower pots through the drainage hole in the bottom of the pot it is advisable always to stand the pots on an ash covered (5 cm deep) area, especially if this area is also dusted with lime as worms will always avoid such materials. A heavy worm population in pots tends to sour the soil which is disadvantageous to carnations.

The best compost for final potting of border carnations into 15 cm pots would be John Innes Compost No. 3. In fact the whole technique of final potting as described for perpetual-flowering carnations (*see* pp. 71–74) can be followed in detail.

There are those cultivars which become established very quickly, whereas others need a considerable amount of assistance. The most vigorous cultivars require a good deal more watering, whereas the sluggish ones must be watered far less. Always remember that root development is greater in drier soil than in over-moist soil. The technique of watering is therefore very much a matter of knowing your cultivars; this can only be gained by experience and careful observation coupled with common sense.

As already mentioned, border carnation plants brought outside during early spring are brought into the greenhouse when the terminal buds are becoming fairly well developed. A good lookout is always necessary to see that the plants outside are not becoming infested with pests such as greenfly.

It has been mentioned before, but border carnations in pots especially should never be disbudded too drastically. Some cultivars will most certainly split the calyx if suddenly all side buds are removed at once. The removal therefore of side growth and side buds from the main flowering stem should be done a few at a time at intervals. Do not remove the uppermost side buds until they are large enough to handle properly without causing damage to the leaves at that node. Any disbudding damage to such leaves will cause the stem to grow sideways, which will make the bloom unsuitable for exhibition purposes.

Hygiene and cleanliness in the greenhouse is of the utmost importance, especially in the case of border carnations.

Second and Subsequent Years — Border Carnations Out of Doors

At the end of the season it is time to tidy up the border carnation border before winter sets in. Clear all surrounding weeds by their roots and cut out all dead or useless weak material. After surrounding trees and shrubs have shed their leaves, clear these away from around the carnation plants as they will encourage slugs and woodlice, both of which will attack and damage carnation plants severely, sometimes fatally. A light dusting of chalk lime around the plants is beneficial and will help to keep slugs at bay, as well as when washed into the soil by autumn rain help to keep the soil sweet.

As soon as spring manifests itself by a general improvement in the weather, and the plants begin to show signs of an increase in vigour, it is time to apply a general top dressing of John Innes Base fertiliser. This should be very lightly scratched into the top of the soil.

The supporting of two-year or older border carnations is made much easier and neater by the use of 'cane-ring' supports. These are wire circular rings which can be easily and simply attached to a single cane fairly close to the plant, and at any given height to encircle the plant's growth just where support is most needed. These supports can be raised or lowered as may be desired and are inconspicuous as well as durable.

During the growing season little additional feeding is necessary, although when plants are making a good deal of vigorous growth an occasional liquid feed with a balance liquid nutritional concentrate, properly diluted, will assist the plant in maintaining health and vigour.

Hardy Garden Pinks

Pinks are totally different from either perpetual-flowering carnations or border carnations. Pinks and borders are equal as far as hardiness is concerned. The south of England is particularly suited to growing pinks to perfection. The climate and the soil, in most places, are almost ideal. I think it is safe to say that the pink, of all *Dianthus*, has given more pleasure to gardeners in many different parts of the world and in many different environments than any other flower. Pinks are fairly easy to grow.

The origin of the pink, as we know the species today, is the varying species of *Dianthus plumarius*. To go into the various kinds of pinks would almost fill a book in itself. Inter-breeding and cross-breeding, over so many years, have produced untold varieties and types. Not only have pink species been used as parent plants for breeding new and improved cultivars, but perpetual-flowering strains have also been used by some growers, hence the variance in character and performance of today's pinks.

Dianthus sinensis was an ancestor of the perpetual-flowering carnation, as indeed was *Dianthus caryophyllus. D. sinensis* and *D. hedewigii* played a great part in the ancestry of pinks. *D. barbalus* is another species which is often mentioned. Today we have the 'laced' pinks which had their popularity in the early nineteenth century. They were sometimes referred to as 'Scotch' pinks. They are recognised by their markings or 'lacing' of the flower colours. 'Dad's Favourite', a very old cultivar, is a typical example of the laced pink. 'Murray's Laced Pink' is another.

Next we have the 'Herbertii' pinks. Very little is known about their origin. Their habit of growth, as well as flowering, somewhat resembles the border carnation. It may well be that the border carnation appeared somewhere in its parentage, although the raiser, Mr C.H. Herbert of Birmingham, has always denied this. 'Bridesmaid' and 'Harmony' are but two of the Herbertii pinks.

191

Another variation is the 'Imperial' pinks. They were raised by that very successful and most knowledgeable grower of pinks and borders, Charles Fielder, with whom I have had the privilege of working while we were both employed on the Wivilsfield Nurseries of Allwood Bros during the years 1927–28. The Imperial pinks produce blooms of exhibition quality and have a habit somewhat similar to Allwoodii pinks, of a perpetual-flowering nature. It is suggested that these plants should be stopped in order to induce the production of strong side shoots.

A few cultivars to mention in this section are: 'Carlotta', a double claret self; 'Crimson Glory', large double ruby crimson; 'Freckles', dusky salmon, flecked red, very dwarf habit; 'Lancing Lass', rose pink with light red eye.

Show Pinks

As implied by their name, these pinks are specifically bred for the show bench, and are the result of crossings between the Old English laced pinks and the Herbertii pinks. Resulting seedlings were crossbred with Allwoodii cultivars, thus giving us these modern aristocrats of the show benches. Culture-wise, there is no difference in requirements. They grow rather taller and the blooms are larger and of perfect form. They flower for longer periods of the year which no doubt is a derivative of their Allwoodii parentage. If show bench perfection is required the plants are best grown in 15 cm pots and require staking in order to support the stem. For exhibition purposes it is best to disbud as recommended for border carnations. They are, however, also worthwhile as garden plants, when they are allowed to grow naturally.

Some cultivars of note are the following: 'Show Achievement', large double flowers, delicate salmon rose with a much deeper centre; 'Show Beauty', large double blooms of rose pink with a maroon eye; 'Show Clove', deep rose-pink, with deep maroon centre, very strongly scented; 'Show Enchantress', large flowers, brick scarlet self; 'Show Ideal', creamy-white double flowers with salmon-red eye.

Alpine Pinks

These are particularly recommended for rockeries, dry walls, or for growing in troughs. Their normal habitat is in pockets of soil of a light texture and well-drained positions. The principal needs, therefore, are an open position with full sunlight. They thrive on soils which are alkaline, so limestone soils would be ideal. Very little fertilisers are needed for these plants as one should prevent the plants becoming too soft and lush. Established plants benefit, however, from a top dressing during early spring, of equal parts coarse sharp sand, sifted rotted-down horse manure or sedge peat and limestone grit, spread around and in between the plants. These pinks originated in the Austrian Alps and they flower mainly in the early summer.

London Pinks

This type of pink was raised by Mr F.R. McQuown. They are the result of cross-breeding and in-breeding using *D. allwoodii* and *D. herbertii* as well as perpetual-flowering carnations as parents. They are vigorous in habit and free-flowering. Several cultivars are beautiful laced. They are easy to grow and are best stopped to produce abundant side shoots.

Some interesting cultivars are the following: 'London Glow', ruby red, edged pink; 'London Girl', semi-double white with lake/carmine lacing; 'London Poppet', white flushed pink, with ruby red lacing, dwarf habit.

Allwoodii Pinks

These truly remarkable pinks were raised by Mr Montague Allwood using the old-fashioned garden pink and the perpetual-flowering carnation, resulting in a type of plant possessing the hardiness, dwarf habit and perfume of the pink, together with the perpetual-flowering habit of the carnation. Some people refer to them as the 'perpetual-flowering' pinks, which is not quite true, although in the south of England it is not uncommon to start cutting flowers from the Allwoodii cultivars in early summer and continue to cut well into the autumn. In fact, at my Sway nurseries, it is often possible to cut blooms of the cultivar 'Doris' or 'Diane' on Christmas Day.

They can be grown in beds, planted 23 cm apart each way and can be carried over for 2 or more years. This has made the Allwoodii cultivars very popular as a commercial proposition as a market cut flower. They can also be grown, apart from edging plants or in the garden border, as plants for garden bowls, troughs, hanging baskets or double walls, window boxes or pots. As for all pinks and carnations, drainage is of the utmost importance, and this applies equally to Allwoodii.

As far as cultural requirements are concerned there is nothing different to that which is recommended for pinks in general.

One point which should be mentioned is that, with Allwoodii especially, the more often the flowers are removed before maturity the more flowers will be produced. Like all pinks they should not be disbudded.

As far as cultivars are concerned, the first one which comes to mind is 'Doris', the most famous pink of our time. It is the most prolific and always in great demand even on the commercial cut flowers markets. The colour is light salmon pink with a deeper salmon eye. 'Diane' is undoubtedly the next best. It is very similar to 'Doris', from which it sported. Its colour is a very deep salmon self. There are a great number of Allwoodii cultivars, but as far as cut flower cultivars are concerned, none are better than the two already mentioned.

Propagation

Pinks are best multiplied by propagation of cuttings. This can be done almost any time from spring until early autumn, although cuttings propagated during mid-summer always seem to make the best plants. There again we must stress the point that only the best, short and sturdy cuttings must be selected from the strongest and most vigorous plants. Do not be tempted to take cuttings which have already commenced to elongate. These, if rooted, will soon run up to flower and do not produce the right type of breaks. They will certainly be less productive.

During mid-summer they may be propagated in pans, pots or boxes in a cold frame, using a mixture of equal parts fine sifted loam, preferably steam sterilised, sharp sand and a good horticultural peat, well mixed. Alternatively, a mix of a fine grade peat with perlite in equal proportions.

For propagation at other times a propagating frame with 'bottom heat' providing a temperature of around 15°C (60°F) in the medium would greatly assist rooting.

194

A question often asked is: 'Do we have to use a rooting hormone powder?' Pinks root fairly easily without the use of hormones, but I would recommend a rooting powder containing a fungicide. The use of this will reduce the risk of damping.

For propagating techniques, *see* pp. 32–60.

Potting

After 4 to 5 weeks the cuttings will be rooted and should be potted up without delay. Once a cutting is well rooted there is nothing gained by leaving it any longer in the propagating medium. As regards potting compost, pots and subsequent treatment of the young plants refer to the potting of borders.

Treatment

Young pink plants, like border carnations, like a well-drained and well-prepared border if planted out in the garden. All subsequent treatment is identical to that as suggested for border carnations. Always avoid planting too deeply. In the south of England it is almost always best to plant in the autumn, while soil conditions are still ideal for a rapid establishment of the young plants.

Spacing of 23 cm from plant to plant is ideal. Always make sure that all plants are adequately moist at the root ball before planting and after planting water-in through a fine rose.

Disbudding and Flower Cutting

Pinks should not be disbudded. When cutting the flowers always use a sharp knife, so as to avoid tugging at the roots of the plant and cut the stem as long as possible in order to keep the plants short and sturdy. Cut the stems just when the terminal bud opens because the side buds will open gradually while in water.

Plants Grown Other than in Borders

It has already been mentioned earlier that pinks can be grown very successfully and produce very charming displays in pots, boxes, bowls, troughs or window boxes, even hanging baskets, but again I have to stress the importance of drainage. A John Innes No. 3 soil would be ideal.

Plants propagated during the summer are grown in small pots

195

This is a pink plant of the Allwoodii type, now well established and beginning to elongate. Here the growing tip is broken out in order to prevent premature flowering.

in a cold frame with plenty of ventilation and during March or early April may be planted out in the window-boxes, pots or troughs. For growing pinks in dry walls or rockeries, one should choose the shorter growing pinks such as 'Winsome', 'Timothy' or 'Freckles'. These do not require any support and would be ideal for such purposes.

Autumn and Winter Treatment

During autumn remove all dead and unsightly growth, old flower stems with spent flowers should be cut low down and straggling growth should be severely shortened.

Hardly any attention is needed during the wintei, except after spells of severe weather and frost. Often young plants are lifted out of the soil by hard frost and these need to be settled down and firmed by gentle treading to prevent the roots from drying. Many pink and border carnation plants are lost each winter season in this way. It is not the frost which kills the plants, but the suspension of the plant and the drying out of the roots which cause the collapse and death of the young plants.

Do not mulch the plants in order to shelter them from frost. This does untold damage by encouraging moisture around the collar of the plant which will cause stem rot apart from the fact that most mulches will encourage wood lice, earwigs and other damage inflicting insects.

When the plants are covered with a thick layer of snow, never attempt to remove this. The plants will not be harmed in any way, in fact the blanket of snow will protect them from the cold winds.

As soon as spring approaches, clean the beds or borders and remove all dead plant material such as leaves, weeds etc from around the plants, and towards the end of March a light dressing of John Innes Base fertiliser at the rate of 55 g per square metre, followed 14 days later by a similar dressing of limestone chippings or chalk lime is all the pink plants require in order to ensure a good show of quality blooms from June onwards.

An occasional insecticide spray, say once a month, is always well worth while as a precaution against insects.

Part III
Descriptions of Cultivars

Numbers refer to colour illustrations.

Perpetual-Flowering Carnations

1   'Arevalo'. Violet/deep purple with pale lavender edges, producing large full flowers on strong erect stems.

2   'Aspinal'. A sport of 'Arevalo', with the same excellent habit, producing large full flowers in deep salmon pink with paling edges.

3   'Astor'. This fast grower produces bright scarlet blooms of high quality, which keep very well. Compact habit, medium height, and seldom splits.

4   'Bailey's Spendour'. Raised on our nurseries, this is still one of the best shell pink varieties. It produces full, well shaped flowers in a pearly pink on plants of medium height, and is ideal for pot culture and the amateur grower: an almost perfect carnation.

5   'Chanel'. Light rose blooms with purple stripes and picotee edging. A very attractive variety which is less susceptible to fusarium.

6   'Clara'. Yellow blooms, edged and flecked with salmon.

7   'Clara's Lass'. White blooms, also edged and flecked with salmon.

8   'Cordoba'. Beautiful crimson flowers carried on long, straight stems; as a cut flower this cultivar has a long vase life. Prolific growth of good quality flowers.

9   'Crowley Sim'. Light salmon pink, this Sim sport is very popular on the commercial flower market. Typical Sim growth.

10 'Dark Pierrot'. A darker lilac sport of 'Pierrot' with picotee edging and stripes, and the same growth habit.

11 'Fragrant Anne'. Large pure white and highly scented blooms on a compact cultivar of medium height. A favourite carnation for exhibition.

12 'Jacqueline Ann'. Strongly scented, this is an excellent exhibition variety and has proved very popular on the show bench. The white blooms are flecked salmon pink.

201

13   'Lena'. This is another Sim sport, a prolific cultivar producing excellent blooms in rich salmon pink with a more intensive colour than 'Laddie Sim'. This strong, robust grower is recommended with every confidence.

14   'Miledy'. An unusual and attractive new shade of rosy pink, this medium height cultivar produces well shaped full flowers on good stems.

15   'Monte Video'. An eyecatching light pink carnation, and an addition of excellent quality to the assortment of pink shades. Long lasting as a cut flower.

16   'Pierrot'. Lavender white with purple edgings and stripes. A most attractive picotee edged variety with excellent growing qualities. Very exclusive.

17   'Raggio di Sole'. A magnificent carnation with a very special colour. Hardly any splitting, and super quality flowers in a rich apricot. Very popular.

18   'Red Runner'. This is an ideal variety for pot culture. Bright scarlet blooms, medium height, compact growth, and it seldom splits.

19   'Roma'. Cream coloured blooms, a strong and prolific grower, and rarely splits.

20   'San Remo'. A new pink standard carnation with deeply serrated petals, and a prolific producer of high quality blooms, this is an exclusive variety.

21   'Valencia'. Another sport of 'Raggio di Sole' with all the same excellent qualities and the same growth habit. The large full blooms are a very attractive golden bronze.

22   'White Sim'. A strong and prolific grower, this variety has been popular for very many years and is still one of the leading white carnations on the commercial flower markets.

Hardy Border Carnations

23   'Bookham Perfume'. Deep crimson blooms, large and well shaped, held on strong erect stems, with an excellent clove perfume. A favourite carnation.

24   'Christine Hough'. A slightly taller cultivar than most. Apricot base colour splashed with cerise rose.

25   'Dainty Lady'. Very fine red pencilling on a pure white ground.

26 'Eva Humphries'. A very old favourite which can still hold its own today. This is a true picotee edged cultivar, camellia white with a delicate edging of purple to the petal edge. A most attractive cultivar indeed.

27 'Fiery Cross'. A very vivid scarlet, an excellent exhibition variety as well as a good garden plant. Strong stems and excellent growth.

28 'Happiness'. Another old favourite which has stood the test of time. Dwarf robust habit, with blooms of an attractive yellow ground, margined scarlet.

29 'Harmony'. A most attractive French grey with cerise markings.

30 'Lavender Clove'. A self lavender colour. Large flowers on excellent stems, with a strong clove perfume.

31 'Lustre'. A cultivar with excellent and robust habit. A rich golden apricot with rosy-pink blush. Strong grower.

32 'Master Stuart'. One of the very first border carnations raised on our Sway nurseries, back in the early 1950's. A dwarf growing cultivar which does not need supports, it produces pure white blooms with bright scarlet pencil markings, on strong stems, and has excellent border habit. Highly recommended by the Royal Horticultural Society after trials at Wisley.

33 'Merlin Clove'. One of the best scented border carnations, white ground, heavily edged and marked with violet-purple.

Pinks

34 'Anniversary'. Raised and introduced by us in 1987, and thus named to celebrate the 50th anniversary of our nursery. A full soft shell pink, with a deeper eye, on strong stems, this is an ideal variety for the border as well as for a patio container.

35 'Betty Webber'. A very attractive cultivar, pink overlaid purple. It was named after Miss B. M. Webber, well known to many of our nursery visitors, as she was with us for more than 25 years in charge of our retail section.

36 'Dad's Choice'. Another of our patio pink introductions, available from spring 1990. A compact grower, pure white ground with a pronounced greenish eye which is surrounded with carmine red. A most attractive variety.

37   'Daily Mail'. A full white with an attractive deep crimson eye.

38   'Doris'. The most outstanding of all the pinks. Raised by the late Monty Allwood and named after his wife Doris, it flowers almost perpetually and is very popular as a cut flower on all the flower markets. In the south of England we cut flowers out in the open from May until late in the year; it is not uncommon to cut some flowers on Christmas Day. Salmon pink, azalea pink eye, semi double.

39   'Granmere Pool'. Raised by Cecil Wyatt, this short growing variety makes tidy plants good for the garden. A very pale pink ground with a deep red/maroon eye.

40   'Haytor's White'. A pure white new cultivar introduced in 1979/80. Excellent for cut flowers as well as attractive in the garden.

41   'Ian'. A very popular glowing crimson double. Strong grower.

42   'Jenny Wyatt'. Another Cecil Wyatt cultivar. This one has pale pink double flowers and is an ideal summer plant.

43   'Nan Bailey'. Raised on our nursery in 1987, and an ideal patio cultivar. At the Royal Horticultural Society Wisley trials it was described as a white self, also perfumed, a very short growing garden plant, still flowering in November.

44   'Paul'. A fine border variety, light rose pink with red speckles and markings.

45   Prudence'. A very dainty cultivar, white ground with ruby lacing.

46   'Sway Belle'. This is one of our 1989 introductions, raised by us at our Sway nurseries. A most attractive cultivar, with a heavily scented white ground, overlaid purple, it is a fast grower, eminently suitable for patio planting.

American Spray Carnations

These charming and graceful varieties are among the most popular cut flowers in the commercial markets of Britain and the continent, carrying as they do several blooms on each flowering stem (see page 160). However, they have not yet been taken up by the amateur carnation grower as enthusiastically as we had anticipated when we introduced the first cultivars from the USA some years ago. The reason for this is difficult to imagine, especially as they have become strong favourites with flower arrangers. There are now many recommended cultivars available, from which we have illustrated the four listed below:

47 'Annelies'. A cream sport of 'Medea', with the same excellent qualities. Fast grower.
48 'Cartouche'. Clear yellow.
49 'Ritmo'. Light pink.
50 'Rony'. An excellent new red. Prolific production of good quality strong sprays, blooms a vivid scarlet.

Appendix

Suppliers of Materials in the UK

Fungicides   Pan Britannica Industries Ltd.,
Waltham Cross, Herts.

Insecticides   Murphy Chemicals Ltd.,
Wheathampstead, Herts.

Smoke-bombs   Plant Protection Ltd.,
Yalding, Kent.

Dusts   Shellstar Ltd.,
70 Brompton Rd., London, SWι.

Chemical sterilisers   Pan Britannica Industries Ltd.

Fertilisers   Fisons Ltd.,
Hartson, Cambridge.

Peat   Fisons Ltd.

Charcoal   Monro Horticultural Sundries Ltd.,
Hertford Road, Waltham Cross,
Herts.

Glasshouses for
carnations   F. Pratten & Co., Ltd.,
Midsomer Norton, Bath, Somerset.

Electrical heating   Consult your local Electricity Board
(Advisory Dept.)

INSECTICIDES

PRODUCT	MANUFACTURER	FORMULATION	PEST CONTROLLED	ACTIVE INGREDIENT
Back to nature spray	PBI	Spray	Greenfly, blackfly, caterpillar, thrips	Rotenone Quassia
Bio Flydown	PBI	Spray	Greenfly, whitefly, red spider, earwigs, woodlice	Permethrin
Abol Derris Dust	ICI	Puffer pack Dust	Caterpillars, greenfly	Rotenone
Abol 'G'	ICI	Spray Partly systemic	Aphids of all kinds	Pirimicarb
Fumite Smoke Cones	ICI	Smoke	Whitefly, red spider, greenfly, leaf miner, thrips, woodlice	Pirimiphos-Methyl
Murphume Smokes	Murphy Chemical Co	Smoke	Aphids, greenfly, thrips	Lindane
Lindex Garden Spray	Murphy	Spray	Aphids, greenfly, thrips, young caterpillars	Gamma-H.C.H.
Systemic Insecticide	Murphy	Spray	Greenfly, whitefly, red spider, and most sap sucking insects	Dimethoate
Rapid	ICI	Spray	Greenfly (quick kill)	Pirmicarb
Sybol 2	ICI	Spray	Especially effective against whitefly Kills by contact and penetrating leaf tissue	Perimiphos-Methyl
Sybol 2 Dust	ICI	Dust	Caterpillars and most common garden pests	Pirimiphos-Methyl
Malathion	PBI	Spray	Whitefly, greenfly, thrips, red spider	Malathion

Product	Manufacturer	Form	Uses	Active ingredient
Rose and Flower Pest Duster	PBI	Dust	Greenfly, red spider, thrips, caterpillars, earwigs, woodlice	Derris and Carbaryl
BIO Systemic Insecticide	PBI	Spray	Greenfly, red spider, thrips and small caterpillars	Dimethoate
Bromophos	PBI	Powder	Soilpests, wireworm, leatherjackets, cutworm	Bromophos
Slug Gard	PBI	Pellets	Slugs, snails, woodlice, leatherjackets	Methiocarb
Murphy's Fentro	Murphy	Spray	*Tortrix*	Fenitrothion
Murphy's Sevin Dust	Murphy	Dust	Caterpillars	Carbaryl
Benlate	PBI	Wettable powder spray	Mildew, *Botrytis*	Benomyl
Liquid Copper Fungicide	Murphy	Spray	Rust, leafspot, fairy ring spot	
Murphy's System Fungicide	Murphy	Spray	Wilt	Thiophanate-Methyl
Bordeay Powder Dithane 945	Murphy PBI	Spray Wettable powder, spray	Rust, spot	Mancozeb
General Garden Fungicide	ICI	Spray	Rust, leafspot, blight, *Botrytis*, mildew	
Orthocide Captan	Murphy	Dust or spray	Rust, powdery and downy mildew, *Botrytis*	Thiram
Hormone Rooting Powder	Murphy	Powder	*Botrytis*, damping off, Fusarium (airborne) Assist rooting of soft wood cuttings containing captan to prevent damping-off	
Hormone Rooting Powder	Boots	Powder	As above.	

209

Mist propagation	MacPenny International Ltd, Gore Road Industrial Estate, New Milton, Hampshire (Tel: 0425 611590).
Irrigation	Access Irrigation Ltd, Crick, Northampton (Tel: 09064 3985).
	Cameron Irrigation Ltd, Harwood Industrial Estate, Littlehampton, Sussex (Tel: 09064 3985).
Heating appliances	Thermal Tempest Engineering Ltd, Yaxley, Peterborough (Tel: 0733 241313).

Metric Conversion Table

1 mm = 0.04 inch
1 cm = 0.4 inch
1 inch = 2.5 cm
1 metre = 3 ft 3 in
1 foot = 0.3 m
1 yard = 0.9 m

1 m² = 10.8 sq ft
1 sq ft = 0.1 m²
1 m³ = 35.3 sq ft
1 cu ft = 0.03 m³

1 acre = 0.4 hectares
1 hectare = 2.5 acres

1 ounce = 28 g
1 pound = 0.5 kg
1 UK gallon = 4.5 l
1 litre = 0.2 UK gallons
1 fl oz = 28 cc
1 US gallon = 3.8 l
1 litre = 0.3 US gallons

Abbreviations

NSA(O) Ltd — Nuclear Stock Association
(Ornamental) Ltd

GCRI — Glasshouse Crops
Research Institute

NPK — Nitrogen/Phosphate/Potash

ppm — Parts per million

Index of Cultivars

Figures in **bold** refer to colour plates.

General Index

214